The Philosophy
of Urban Existence

Wur I tew bee gyvn a faire cytee
whereyn tu taik mye stande, I could,
deare Sire, moov ye wurlde.

—FANEBIUS PERLYNG

The Philosophy of Urban Existence

A PROLEGOMENON

A. K. BIERMAN

Being a tract on the Good Life, Concinnation, The One and the Many, City-States (Now), The Creation of Persons, Immanence and Transcendence, Understanding, Moral Power, Sense of Community, Neighborhoods, Justice and Tolerance, Points of View, The Arts and Their Detrivialization, Urban Dialectic, Work, Leisure, and an Art Force

Ohio University Press

I dedicate this book to Rod Lundquist, without whose . . . and to June Dunn, with whose . . . and to Becky Jenkins, by whose . . . and to Jack Morrison, because of whose . . . and Don Santina and Richard Reineccius, in whose . . .

Preface

Lately, I have been anxious to move philosophy out of the academy and into the world, closer to the chaos. This essay is one of my moves in that fearsome direction. Wrestling with the chaos, trying to shape it for the comfort of man, is the ultimate challenge to the worth of philosophy.

This is a philosophical essay on the city and the good life. As such, it falls on the theoretical side of thought more than on the practical side, but if it were to become operative theory, it would engender many practical changes. The practical aspects of urban existence and the discussion of urban problems have come into academic, journalistic, and political prominence. Mayors, Congress, sociologists, demographers, anthropologists, engineers, ecologists, economists, psychologists, technocrats, planners, artists, communes, politicians, citizens, cranks, businessmen, and urbanologists make the news, write tracts, propose solutions, lay plans, produce studies, statistics, surveys, analyses, maps, and criticisms, formulate demands and projects, scheme schemes and dream dreams. I find the mass of these productions dreary, narrow, dated, jerry-built, money-bound, and visionless. In this essay, you will not find statistics, surveys, maps, tax-sharing plans, and so forth of that kind. All such desiderata are inconclusive, contradictory, partial, which defects can be eliminated only after we widen the scope and deepen the perspective with a philosophical vision of the city. This essay is an attempt to create such a philosophical vision.

I do not say it is a philosophical essay to forewarn you but to lure you on. Do not turn away because you think philosophy is not your forte; it is. At least, the philosophy of this essay is your forte because its central philosophic topic is the good life, one to which every mature person has given some thought.

The first chapter sketches the background of historically important conceptions of the good life and places the prevailing notion of the good life that contemporary Americans have in that context. The second chapter proposes what modern man's vocation should be if he is to live the good life. The third chapter argues that the social and political locus of man's life should be the city-state rather than the nation-state. The remainder of the chapters address themselves to the nature of persons, the kind of moral-political conditions that must obtain in cities if they are to be a congenial environment for the human spirit, and the role that the arts and philosophy can and must play if we are to escape the moral, political, and cultural sewer in which we presently wade chartlessly about.

In this essay, I do not propose the means by which captive cities are to free themselves from their national gaols, nor do I sketch organization charts for city-state governments, nor do I outline the massiveness of the political and economic changes entailed by a move from nation-states to city-states, nor do I design specific civic machinery to utilize the civilizing balm of the arts and philosophy that I claim are needed to construct the good civic life. We design the machine we intend to make before we design the tools with which to make it; likewise for social and political machinery. First things first.

What I have to say in this essay can be considered independently of the controversies in which proponents of capitalism, the welfare state, or socialism are typically embroiled. Whatever economic arrangements prevail for a population, each economic system would have to consider the issues I write about in this essay. It is encouraging, however, to note that both Ernest Che Guevara and Mao Tse-tung have given philosophical thought to creating the social conditions that can bring forth a "new man." Neither holds the view that once the "capitalist rascals" are thrown out and the "socialist heroes" are installed in power the revolution is secured and finished. For them, the political revolution is only a prelude to the cultural revolution, which is aimed at producing the "new man."

In my mind, Guevara and Mao are in the right ball park, but they do not re-think the concept of man deeply or radically enough. Recognizing the commendable effort at decentralization in Mao's China, my analysis of the concept of person leads me to conclude that the city-state is the form of polity best suited to achieving the good life. I do not believe Guevara's aim—for man to realize his social being—is attainable outside the city-state. Nation-states, for example, are wholly absorbed in solving the Brobdingnagian problems that their own massiveness has itself produced. Modern man in the West is fractured, wasted, morally confused, alienated, insecure, self-centered, and socially aimless. In reading this essay, you will see, given the nature of persons that I outline herein, why neither nation-states, nor trans-national "economic communities," nor internationalism in any form, legal or economic, can make you whole, or revive your zest for living, or integrate you and restore your sense of community.

It's time we were moving on. It's time to start for the promised land. Man is born free; and everywhere he is in nations. "Stadtluft macht frei"—City air makes men free.

Before releasing you to the essay, I hasten to say that it is a prolegomenon to a more fully developed philosophy of urban existence. I find it advisable to print some prolegomena philosophy of urban existence now for three reasons: First, I sense that the hearts and thoughts of our countrymen—certainly their bodies—are hastening to urban loci and I want them to take some philosophy with them. Secondly, since no one by himself can comprehend fully the city nor speak for its people, I hope to enlist a cooperative readership through this essay so that together we can philosophically advance toward a fuller philosophy. Thirdly, a fully worked out philosophy of urban existence addressed to professional philosophers would be too elaborate for the larger public who, under the press of getting on with their work, will find a prolegomenon more useful to them; and it is the larger public that is presently uppermost in my mind.

Contents

1   THE GOOD LIFE

Ohhh! Tew bee alyve agayn!
—FANEBIUS PERLYNG

All rational men wish to live the good life, and wish to do that which in their time and place is most likely to produce the good life. My thesis in this chapter is that Americans tend to embrace the self-realization theory of the good life rather than other traditional theories, and, except for the wave makers, they advocate self-realization through work.

❁   ❁   ❁

WE ALL SHALL DIE. It is useful to remind ourselves of this from time to time because it is absurdly easy to waste our days on earth. Thinking on the-end-of-it-all serves marvelously well to concentrate our minds on how to get our time's worth here. The thought of death is hard enough to bear without also being haunted by a sense of waste, waste, waste.

What is the good life?

Some say with Aristotle that it is a life marked by happiness. Others say with the Stoics that it is a life lived in accordance with virtue, deaf to the yelps of desires whose fulfillment is dependent upon fortune and the cooperation of others.

Still others say with Augustine and Aquinas that the good life starts with death when our souls are fully occupied in communion with God. Kant says that the good life is the moral life, one in which we perform our duties; being worthy of happiness is a higher good than happiness. Still others say that the good life is one in which we realize to the fullest our human capacities, a life of self-realization.

Philosophy always stands in the dock under suspicion because, on any question, one can find philosophers who disagree in their answers. This seems to be true whether we survey the history of philosophy or whether we take the measure of contemporary philosophers. One question and several answers: The question: What is the good life? The several answers: Happiness, living in accordance with virtue, contemplating God, doing our duty, and self-realization. What are we to think of an enterprise as riven with dissension as philosophy is?

Three things may be said in the defense of philosophy.

First, the reputation of philosophy should not be smirched because it isn't arithmetic. In doing both of them we reason and think and infer; so far, they are alike. But arithmetical questions have one and only one answer; if two arithmeticians produce different answers for the same question, one or both of them has reasoned incorrectly. We appraise arithmetical answers by saying that they are "wrong" or "incorrect" or "right" or "correct." Philosophical answers are not arithmetical statements, and, so, must be appraised differently. Instead of saying that a philosopher's answer is right or wrong, we should say that it is reasonable or unreasonable. Since various answers to a single philosophical question may all be reasonable, we are not justified in saying of the various philosophers as we would of arithmeticians that one or all are wrong, that one or all have reasoned incorrectly.

Differing answers to philosophical questions should not panic us into taking a poll or a vote to decide, for example, about the good life. Reasoning about the good life is not discredited by the fact that more than one view is reasonable. When reasonable men differ about the good life, at least they have reasonable differences and reasonable results, and that is good. We take heart, therefore, and proceed to philosophize about the good life, confident that careful reasoning about the good life will produce a reasonable result.

A second thing to be said in defense of philosophy is that a philosophical answer given in one circumstance may not be as reasonable as another in different circumstances. Thus, historically, because philosophers lived in varying circumstances, we should not be surprised that they gave different answers to the same question. Aristotle lived in a state where men had confidence in the efficacy of government; the Stoics' unsanforized life circumstances shrank their confidence in governments and other men; Kant thought during a period and in a place where stern, Christian doctrine exerted a strong influence. Men and philosophers cut their sail to suit the wind; it is absurd to say such-and-such is the good life when circumstances make it impossible or incapable of attainment.

My own views in this essay are framed in response to what I conceive to be the greatest present and future changes in urban circumstances.

Thirdly, in defense of philosophy, the existence of a variety of answers to a philosophical question may be explained by the fact that what appears by its wordly form to be a single question may not really be a single question. One may understand a question sentence in one way, another man in another way.

As a case in point, we take the one in hand. "What is the good life?" has been taken in each of the following ways: What is the good way to be? What should man do on earth? What are the best things to have? Where it appears that we have one question, there are actually at least three, and these three invite different kinds of answers.

To "What is a good way to be?" one might answer serene, pleased, satisfied, or happy. They are not appropriate answers to "What should men do on earth?"; to this last question we might appropriately answer work, contemplate, perform your duties, or concinnate. And we are familiar with several answers which have been given to "What are the best things to have?", answers such as food and shelter, health, reputation, fame, peace of mind, and wealth.

While we cannot fully say what the good life is without considering how we should be, what we should do, and what we must have, I shall concentrate my reasoning in this essay on what we should do. I begin by sketching typical urban, American attitudes toward the vocations recommended by the various philosophic schools I mentioned at the beginning of this chapter.

The majority of Americans have not flirted seriously with Aristotle's suggestion that what man should do is contemplate. They haven't been seduced even though Aristotle flatteringly reminded us that to contemplate is to exercise that faculty which is unique to man, a faculty which sets him apart from and above the other animals. Rather, we are pragmatically oriented. For us, thinking has been valued more as a prelude to action than as something of value in its own right. Most of the thinking we do is in the service of work.

The American experience is growing alien to Stoic self-restraint. Our doing no longer puts its weight in the service of clamping the lid on the life of our body and its desires. Instead of retreating from life because we fear disappointment, we have energetically said "Yea" to life, and as inheritors of the industrial revolution and its technological wonders, we elbow each other all the way to the cornucopia.

The denizens of American cities have been a disappointment to the followers of Augustine and Aquinas. We have dared to keep our eyes on our piece-work rather than on God. We are a here-and-now people. The advance pitchmen for

God have not filled their tents with many who hunger chiefly for communion with God here or in the hereafter. God helps those who help themselves, right, Parson? Although we stand in need of grace to get our tickets to heaven, knowing full well that good works alone are insufficient, Americans have acted as if hard work will do the job. Aquinas' insight that virtue lies in the good, not in the difficult *per se*, has been generally ignored.

Despite the fact that with Kant we may piously applaud worthiness above happiness and that we may occasionally advocate the performance of duty as our highest vocation, we betray our true attitude in our despair of some consequences which follow upon a strenuous, though necessarily doomed, effort to live the dutiful, moral life. The consequences are a life riddled with regret and guilt. Severe guilt and regret produce painful neuroses or disabling psychoses; we are urged on all hands to get medical help from psychiatrists, psychologists, group therapy sessions, or drugstore palliatives to restore the mental and emotional equilibrium so necessary to resume our "inalienable" pursuit of "life, liberty, and happiness."

We urban Americans are not avid affirmers of Kant's vision; we do not live a life in accordance with duties; we live a regulated life. We seldom consciously choose an action because it optimally fulfills our duty; mostly we conform out of habit. That is the reality of our behavior. Thus, where there might be free choice guided by moral imperatives, we usually have constraint by regulation; where we might find purging pain in guilt and regret when we do not do our duty, we harbor sullen resentment of those who promulgate and execute constricting regulations. We are hedged, harried, and bedeviled by statutes, regulations, rules, restrictions, prohibitions, orders, memos, directives, and resolutions issuing continually from upper rungs of a hierarchically structured society; because we have had so little part to play in the formulation of the regulations, we do not embrace them as positive expressions of our moral aspirations but only resent them as the tools of control and repression by "those" who would use us for their own purposes.

Kant's community of free, equal, moral agents is American neither in reality nor in desire. We live by regulations instead of moral imperatives and we are not granted the moral guilt necessary to the existence of a Kantian community.

Although most Americans have not taken to the vocations recommended by Aristotle, the Stoics, Aquinas, or Kant, it is important to realize that they do not wholly reject them either. Each of them is contained to some extent in our common sense notions of the good life. At times each of us appreciates the value of contemplation, faces up to the necessity of self-denial, yearns to merge with something outside himself, and recognizes the pull of duty.

Of the several views of what we should do to live the good life, an "individualist" version of the self-realization theory is the one most nearly acceptable to urban Americans. Americans wish "to get ahead," to better ourselves. Most of us feel that we should realize our potential and give thought to future personal growth. We wish to actualize our potentialities. The typical way to do this is by working. Of course, some work actualizes our potentialities better than other work does. What we do to realize a better self is to get educated so we can advance to better jobs. We prepare ourselves for and assume greater responsibilities in a society whose chief organizational device is a hierarchical structure. In that kind of society, education prepares us to move up the hierarchical scale, and promotion does it in fact.

Responsibility increases as we move up in hierarchical status, and with increased responsibility we achieve increased significance and worth. More of our abilities are engaged. To be at the bottom of the hierarchy is to have little worth, little self-respect, and few responsibilities.

The self-realization ideal in a hierarchical society is a comfortable home for personal ambition, a familiar driving force behind the individualistic grasp for self-realization. Relations between persons are saturated with competitiveness, and we salve our faint concern for those whom the struggle leaves on the lower rungs with the implicit, comforting assumption that not everyone is equally apt material for full realization. Some of us are burlap and others of us are silk. Overemphasis on individualistic self-realization, where self-realization is defined in the rugged, competitive terms appropriate to a hierarchical society, tends to foster selfishness and patronization.

There is also a "statism" version of self-realization. It is meant to mask the disparity in individual self-realization between those at the bottom and those at the top of the hierarchy, and thus, hopefully, avoid revolt against and consequent dismantling of the hierarchical society. It rejects, rightly, the concept of atomistic, rugged individualism; it maintains that the identity of the self is achieved by, in F. H. Bradley's formulation, "sharing with others the relations of the social state," and glorifies the worth of those on the lower rungs by emphasizing the necessity of every role's contribution to the good state. Necessity is a leveler because, presumably, there are no degrees of necessity.

No one, according to statism self-realization theories, is worthless; each one has his "station and his duties." Each station is essential and each person in each station is to feel the worth and responsibility of being essential to the healthy whole. In this theory of self-realization, we are to realize ourselves by performing the duties of our station; in performing our duties, we will realize the state, and, consequently, realize ourselves since our identity depends on the state.

"My station and its duties" is super-patronizing. It is an all-life sucker for lower-runged persons. It is the apotheosis of a hierarchical society, where the citizens' regimental status is cleverly hidden from them by the civilian garb with which the state clothes them in peacetime. Few Americans, especially those on the lower rungs, take kindly to being told *a la* Hegel that they are "a pulse-beat of the whole system, and [themselves] the whole system."

No conception of the good life has a serious chance of taking explicit root in the American, urban mind which frames a vocation for man out of hierarchical timber. Any vocation whose practice can give us the dignity and worth of self-realization must be sold as equally available to all regardless of our occupational and monetary station. And, truly, the good life, citizens, cannot be dispensed in ratios defined by a hierarchical order.

In review: Over against Aristotle's contemplation, Americans have placed practicality; against Stoic self-denial, we have placed the exploitation of technology and consumption; against the deferred promise of heavenly communion with God we have placed here-and-now work; against Kant's performance of duty, we have placed reluctant, smarting conformity with regulations; and rather than being aced into a Germanic, fawning statism version of self-realization, we have plumped for individualist, competitive self-realization *via* hierarchical advancement.

In reasoning our way to the good life, the traditional American material we confront is practicality, consumption, technology, work, regulations, and upward mobility. Chief and central in this material is work; work has been the American vocation. Work is what we do to realize our potentialities. Work requires practical thinking; the rewards of work are more and more goods to consume; machines are obedient partners in productive work; the American production and distribution system, wherein we spend our alert, productive, daylight hours, is a semi-military hierarchy; and regulations are the bonds holding that system together.

Nothing I've said so far about the American response to

historically important philosophies of the good life is new. I have simply tried to state the obvious, what we have all observed and what the popular journals, magazines, and newspapers have reflected. I want to get down in general terms in one place what our predominant present life attitudes and circumstances are. I haven't as yet acknowledged that there are waves on the waters. That comes next.

2 THE VOCATION OF MAN AND HOW TO GO TO BED WITH THE MACHINE IN EDEN

I herd a wumman ynne the Strande saye, "Yt gyves purpos tew mye lyf, and mye 'usbande don't mynd."

—FANEBIUS PERLYNG

Concinnation is the proper vocation for anyone who wishes to lead the good life. Since to concinnate is to lead the good life, every wise man's life is an attempt to return to Eden and a life of leisure so that he may concinnate continually and uninterruptedly.

🏵 🏵 🏵

BEFORE CONSORTING with our native wave makers and divining what new directions they portend, I want to place our present circumstances in a sweepingly simple, mythical perspective.

Man's vocation on earth is to find his way back to Eden.

In a well known Mediterranean myth, Adam and Eve lived in idyllic Eden. They ate of the fruit of the forbidden tree and were cursed by God. He cursed them in two ways: He gave Adam and Eve stomachs and reproductive organs. Since their exit from Eden, Adam has been cursed to work for his and his family's stomachs and Eve has been cursed to ache in, of, and by her womb, and together they made more of us who have had to cope with producing the necessities of life and with each other. This is a familiar cycle.

> Unto the woman he said, I will greatly multiply thy sorrow and thy conception; in sorrow thou shalt bring forth children . . .
> And unto Adam he said, . . . In the sweat of thy face shalt thou eat bread, till thou return unto the ground; for out of it was thou taken: for dust thou art, and unto dust shalt thou return.

Since Adam and Eve were thrown into the jail of the world, their descendants have tried to bend a circular, return route to Eden, that utopia of the mind where the good life was lived. The first arc of that wandering search for the good life has been marked chiefly by their struggle with nature, the mother of their necessities. They have been cursed to concentrate primarily on the third of the three questions into which we divided "What is the good life?", namely, "What are the best things to have?" Americans are no exception.

Consumption is a necessity; the stomach will be served! The good life requires some food, drink, shelter, skills, education, and money. Man's need to procure these necessities, in turn, dictates his vocation: Work. And that is an answer to the second of the three questions, "What should man do on earth?".

More Americans are closer to Eden than the mass of citizens of most nations on earth. This great productive, machine-America has all the means of providing what men must have to lead the good life. America, in being materially closer to Eden, is thereby closer to a philosophic crisis. We will be among the first able to enter the next arc on the return route to Eden, and that means we shall be the first to face the choice of a new vocation. John Henry and Paul Bunyon, America's folk heroes, those prodigious workers, will have to be replaced by new heroes.

Sylvia Porter, the financial page columnist, cites a research council's projection of trends in leisure time. By 1985—just one year after 1984—a worker in the United States will have to choose either (a) to double his present earnings or (b) to take a 25-week vacation, work a 22-hour week, and retire at age 38.

That choice puts our philosophic crisis squarely before you. Are you going to continue working full-time or are you going to cut your income so you can spend more time pursuing another (probably non-paying) vocation? Are you going to stay on the first arc of the return to Eden or are you going to move on to the next arc?

Staying on the first arc, doubling your earnings, means an affirmation of practical thinking, technology, consumption, work, regulations, and a race for the top rungs. We are familiar with that choice; that's where we live. But what is in store for us if we choose the second arc?

To be freed of the first arc is to be freed of the tyranny of our stomachs, but that doesn't free us from the plentitude of Eve's womb. I suggest that the next arc is a struggle, not with nature, but with the city. That is where most of the people are; that is the arena where we shall practice our next vocation. That is where we shall concinnate.

Before I indicate the nature of concinnation, our new vocation, I want to silhouette the wave makers who are ruffling the American pond with waves of contradictions. By sketching in some contradictions haunting American cities, I hope to heighten the sense of immediacy which should attend the impending philosophic crisis. In addition, reflection on the contradictions will help us capture the nature of the transition from the first to the second arc.

Contradiction 1: Practical thinking. Corporations are discovering that the number of college graduates who want management jobs in American industry is declining in proportion to our population. There is no more congenial environment for practical thinking than American industry. J. J.

Servan-Schreiber, the eminent French editor and writer, points this out. He has warned Europeans that they can never hope to compete with America until they reform their schools and corporate structure to train their youth for and to use the efficient management techniques of American industry and business. But, while America acknowledgedly outdistances others on the first arc, partly because of its emphasis on practical thinking, our college graduates are turning their backs on it, shifting to graduate schools, the liberal arts, government service, teaching, and research.

Contradiction 2: Consumption. The pain of not consuming is death, and the price of consuming is work. Work is the vocation forced on us by the necessity of consumption. Now, just when we have the technological means to reduce the amount of work we must do, American advertising genius has peaked its ability to create new consumption "necessities," thereby pricing us back to work. The American market has an astonishing ability to produce and market something for the "person who has everything." Hyped-up consumption hungers are an albatross around our stomachs. You really don't need to have that bellybutton lint remover to lead the good life.

Contradiction 3a: Work. While fat dowagers rail at "the lazy, shiftless welfare leeches" because of their supposed aversion to work, those same dowagers respond enthusiastically to an automobile manufacturer's pitch that "power accessories take the work out of driving." They also hire maids, buy disposals, install automatic garage door openers, have food sent in, and buy exercising machines to take the exercise out of exercising.

Americans are confused about work.

Contradiction 3b: Work. While minorities are knocking themselves out to get jobs and work, hippies and their overground and underground heirs, in an effort to live the life of leisure, are turning away from a workaday place in America. Minority struggles to gain civil justice and economic equality are essentially conservative. Minorities simply want what most Americans have had; they want their now and their future to resemble the white man's affluent past. But hippies and communers are more radical; they are the anti-work emissaries of the new leisure who have "better things to do" than work. In their search for a new vocation, they split into two camps, those on a trip of self-discovery, with the aid of drugs, and/or religion, and those who are socially oriented, who want to construct a new community undominated by the juggernaut of commerce.

While minorities want the independence, confidence and self-reliance that a good job brings, the hippies see a job as castrating and destructive of independence. They have lost confidence in the importance of mercantilism. Spend your days fitting shoes on choosy ladies and squirmy kids?! Forget it! Self-reliance isn't achieved when you're tied to some shoe manufacturer's budget.

Americans are not of one mind about work.

Contradiction 4a: Technology. Farm technology has forced rural Blacks and other farm workers from the country to the city where technology has made it difficult for them to get jobs. Just at the point where we could begin to love the machine because it can begin to produce plenty, our economic system, in maldistributing that plenty, has made the machine an object of resentment.

Contradiction 4b: Technology. The American creed has been successfully instilled: Be industrious for industry; work harder to do better; measure success by a workstick. And now Sylvia Porter suggests that there won't be that much work. How can you love the machine that will make your instilled value system, and old-fashioned you, obsolete?

Contradiction 4c: Technology. Work is a curse God laid on Adam. Relief and Eden are in sight because our technology is improving our machines to the point where they can do the work with which we are now cursed. Thank God for machines! But as machines more and more do what we do, a disturbing, profound suspicion is spreading amongst us: Are we, after all, mere machines, that machines can do what we do? Curse machines that have eaten of the Tree of Knowledge! Unless we can learn to go to bed with the machine in Eden, it will be our dehumanizer rather than our benefactor.

Contradiction 5: Regulatory democracy. While more and more of our life becomes regulated, while the federal government has extended its departments and bureaus into more state, county, and city affairs than in any previous period of our history, the demand for citizen participation in government grows. Neither students, nor the poor, nor shell-back Republicans want government by representation; they want to do it themselves. Evergrowing liberal, progressive legislation designed for the little people has, paradoxically, miniaturized them further. The giant's feet are sticking out from under the midget's bedclothes.

Contradiction 6: Hierarchical ascension. The ideal of egalitarian democracy has always been frustrated by our actual veneration of the men at the top of our hierarchy. America has always made promises to everybody and touted the "common man," but reserved the pay-off for the winners. Yet, there are so many who have kept the faith.

We are now in a position to think our way out of the philosophic crisis generated by the contradictions. One side of each contradiction belongs to the arc of the past and the other belongs to the arc of the future. Urban America's new arc is graphed by the path of its contradictive rebound from a creaking creed.

The new arc pits theoretical thinking against practical

thinking, participation against regulation, a lesser work load against a doubled salary, restraint against acquisitiveness, and a loving admiration for the machine against a cowering apprehensiveness about human adequacy. The old values rotate like planets around the sun of work; as that sun sets in the west, its planets set with it. But what new sun has the character to be the center of the new values? What is the fitting vocation of the future? That philosophical question is as easy to master as a shark in our bathtub.

I have already telegraphed my answer to this question. The new vocation is concinnation. The word comes from a Latin root; to concinnate means to join fitly or becomingly together, make well-connected; choose and compose suitably. I suggest that we poor, cursed things from Eve's womb are the material we should concinnate. Concinnation is a moral vocation. The highest vocation of us who approach the second arc is to concinnate ourselves into the republic of an urban Eden.

Life has come to be and will be even more an urban affair. Cities are the main sites of life. The "Garden of Eden" is a dated re-run from the past, a long vanished coconut community, nevermore to be. The "Garden" is so remote from normal living that a question which gave delightful free play to the speculative imagination of the church fathers still has tickle-power; that question was "What did Adam do in the Garden of Eden before the Fall?" Today, it is realistic to speak only of the "City of Eden" rather than the "Garden of Eden."

What Adam did before the Fall seems an idle, though wonderful, question, just because doing is understood as a normal response to a need, and it is hard to specify just what needs Adam could have had in the Garden. If doing is undertaken to satisfy a need, the chief doing is what is done to satisfy the most urgent need. I shall argue that our present most urgent human need is for social consolidation through unification of the city. Our awareness of that need surfaces painfully in our personal, emotional lives: It surfaces as alienation and such associated plagues as isolation, feelings of social ineffectiveness and aimlessness, as truncated benevolence and excessive self-centeredness, in the agony of insecurity stemming from the absence of socially confirmed and shared convictions, in frustration at being unable to experience the release that follows uninhibited commitment, in our moral confusion wrought by contradictory impulses and goals, in ungrounded suspicions and fears, and consequent shame for our reluctant withdrawal from civic existence.

This pitiful pathology of our emotional lives is not traceable to psychological inadequacies, nor to personal failings, nor to original sin, nor to existential anxieties; therefore, it cannot be treated successfully by psychological counselling, nor by personal reform, nor by religious revival or the importation of Eastern religions, nor by philosophical fads. This pathology is traceable mainly to the fact that we do not live in morally whole civic communities; thus, the only cure for these pathological emotional plagues is a moral and social one: We must make our cities creative, supportive, moral resources in our pursuit of the good life of self-realization, recognizing that the person-self is a social entity, as I shall show in Chapter 7. That persons are social entities means that we should opt for a social version of self-realization achievable by concinnation rather than for the first-arc, individualistic, American version achievable by competitive work.

I advocate the vocation of concinnating in this essay because it is a doing whose purpose is to unify cities and morally to consolidate their citizens, and, thereby, to restore our emotional health by banishing alienation and its associated plagues, and to create unified, realized persons.

Before proceeding further, it will help you to follow my argument in this essay if I give you a "flow chart" that structures the main factors involved in my proposal for concinnating our way to the good civic life. Following the flow chart is an explanation of it, including a summary relating of the chapters subsequent to the flow chart. I hope the chart, its explanation, and chapter summaries will help you to structure your understanding of this essay on urban existence. They give you a map to consult in case you lose the thread of the argument, or want to anticipate what is coming.

The explanation of the flow chart factors does not follow in the strict numerical order I have given them.

1. *Citizen's concinnation.* This is where the first two chapters have brought us. I have stated that this essay is about the good life and, rather than addressing how we should be or what we should *do* to live the good life, I have pointed out that Americans traditionally have advocated work as the vocation of man, and I have exposed some contradictions between a passing creed and a coming one now forming in our society. Opting for the coming creed because it is the second arc on our return to Eden, I recommended that concinnation rather than work be the vocation of the good life, that concinnation be practised in cities because that is where the people are, and will increasingly be in the future.

Concinnation is a social vocation leading to social self-realization and, as such, runs obliquely to the work vocation by which most Americans achieve individualistic self-realization. I do not think Americans can be persuaded to give up their individualistic cast until they understand that it is based on a metaphysical theory of persons that reduces man to the status of an object. I undermine that theory in Chapter 6, and in Chapter 7 go on to replace it with an analysis of the concept of person that shows we are social beings. My analysis is a logical one and my claim a metaphysical one, not the trite empirical and empirically based claim that we are influenced by and become human because of our social environment. Because the nature of our social being is not philosophically understood, we have a naive grasp of the effects

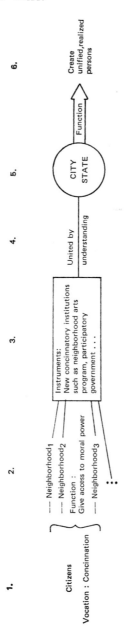

that inadequate social organization has on us; consequently, we suffer now the pathology of alienation and its associated plagues that I have just described. In Chapter 8, I use my theory of persons to explain the concept of alienation in its most general form and to show that this alienation cannot be cured except by unifying the society in which man, the social being, is to live out his days.

5. *City-state.* Because the city is the only form of polity that I believe we can successfully unify, and thereby cure man's alienation, I advocate the return to the city-state. In the next chapter, I show why it would be wise to abandon the nation-state.

Because the unity of the city is a necessary condition for curing man's ailing social nature, we are confronted with the ancient philosophical issue of the One and the Many: Given that some entities, including cities, are complex and, thus, consist of Many parts, how may the Many parts become One? The city being a complex entity, we have to supply an account of its unity. Chapter 4 is devoted to the discussion of the issue of the One and the Many; and, in Chapter 5, I review and reject various theories of social unity that have been advocated. In Chapter 8, I use the novel as a guide in my search for the principle of civic unity. This leads me to consider the city as a work of art in Chapter 10.

6. *Function of the city-state.* By considering the city as a work of art, we are to think of it as end-functional rather than as means-functional. A hammer is means-functional; it is a means of helping us produce something else, and to do that it must be in existence prior to the end product; government is also means-functional. A work of art is end-functional; it is not a means used to make its product because it arrives in existence simultaneously with its product. A city, too, comes into existence simultaneously with its product.

A city's function is to create unified, realized persons; that function is performed when it is unified because simultaneously its citizens, too, are unified into realized existence.

Our experience of a unified work of art has a specific character. So does our experience of a unified functioning city; its character is experienced as a dynamic sense of community (Chapter 10). This experience is our awareness that we are cured of social alienation and its associated plagues.

Although I argue that we should seek social self-realization rather than individualistic self-realization, my view does not imply that the "self" is lost, submerged, or downgraded. I celebrate the glory of the self in Chapter 9 where it is shown how the self may miraculously gain its freedom from nature's bonds and, by paradoxically transcending itself, remake itself. We do this by fashioning a functioning city that is thoughtfully, deliberately designed to sustain the kind of person we wish to be.

2. Neighborhoods and their function. In Chapter 4, I identify neighborhoods as a city's essential parts and, because I believe that our sense of community must be a dynamic one, I find that the function of neighborhoods is to give people access to power. In achieving unity, we should not lose neighborhood diversity nor shun conflict; however, to make dynamic concinnating an equal contest, each person must have an equal access to peaceful power. This peaceful power I identify as moral power and explain and give examples of it in Chapter 12.

4. Understanding. Moral power is exercised to infuse an understanding of our point of view about life into other persons. I discuss the concept of understanding in Chapter 11, and in Chapter 13 explain why moral power enables us to harvest a social point of view from our understanding of differing personal and neighborhood points of view. A social point of view is single and held in common by citizens; being single, it is one; as a commonly held one, it is that which unifies (one-ifies) a city, ties a city's neighborhood parts together. With unity achieved through the exercise of moral power, we inherit the two chief civic virtues of justice and tolerance.

3. *Instruments.* Citizens must have institutional instruments to use in practising their concinnating vocation. Our present institutions are social instruments that were created during the first arc on the circling return to Eden. They were devised primarily to produce or to encourage and buttress the effort of producing what we must have to live the good life. Those institutions—business, industry, schools, the church, government, and the professions—were designed to train and encourage people to work, to deify work, and to provide work. They were not designed to prepare people for or to provide them with concinnating tasks. In setting out on the second arc, the great challenge awaiting us—the great challenge to practical thinking—is the creation of new institutional instruments that can provide meaningful activity for those adults who in selecting restraint over acquisitiveness will have that 25 week vacation, 22 hour work-week, and no working vocation after age 38. We must provide concinnatory possibilities and instruments for them.

Among them are two such instruments, one providing citizens access to art and the other to philosophy, because as I show in Chapter 14, the arts can be detrivialized by becoming a civic means of infusing understanding; and in the last chapter, Chapter 15, I explain the role that philosophy can play in unifying cities through its dialectical process of concinnating conflicting points of view into a social point of view. In the Appendix, I give a short account of a neighborhood arts program, an instrument I helped design for San Francisco, and which serves as an example of a new concinnatory institution.

Given my contrast of the first and second arcs of our return to Eden, it will be obvious to the reader that the economic arrangement now prevailing in our cities still chains us need-

lessly to the first arc. Only a better exploitation of our techni-
cal production possibilities and a more equitable distribution
of our affluence could free us from the first arc, launch us on
the second, and thereby free us to practice the more ennobling
vocation of concinnation. The development of this economic
theme lies outside the scope of this essay.

I proceed to the argument I have just outlined, starting in
the next chapter with an attack on the nation-state, which I
regard as the main political obstacle to the founding of city-
states.

3 TOWARD THE SOVEREIGNTY OF CITIES

I am as loathe tew Pressydents
as I am tew Kynges.
—FANEBIUS PERLYNG

My thesis in this chapter is that cities—including mine, San Francisco—should sever their entangling foreign alliances with their states and the United States. They should become city-states. San Francisco, for example, could become an international city of peace, a haven of ivory and gold on the rim of the great Pacific bowl. Other cities could develop their special qualities and advantages unhindered.

❁   ❁   ❁

My FIRST unabashed public profession that I favored a return to the city-state because it is the best form of government was made on June 23, 1962 in the *Honolulu Star-Bulletin*. In an article for that paper, I argued that the bloated size of political units is regrettable. I realize that to promote a return to the city-state is to swim uphistory, but I still think it a tenable position and shall present several arguments which show it is not a frivolous recommendation.

The social disease that has proved most virulent in modern times is nationalism. Considering that the major advantage which nations enjoy over other existing social units is their ability to wage incredibly destructive wars, nationalism has become a foaming, menacing madness. This single fact is sufficient to wholly discredit the continuing existence of nations. Unfortunately, the obviousness of this social disease has not motivated citizens to disband their nations; I realize that my frontal assault here on the concept of a nation is not likely to move them either; it may have no more effect on them than the technique of immersing a madman in ice water has on him; the shock gives him pause, momentarily silences his raving but does not effect a cure. The cure will come only when citizens have positive reasons for transferring their master loyalty from the nation to another social unit. I maintain that the social unit to which they owe their master loyalty is their city. This essay as a whole may be construed as an extended argument for that.

There are several social units to which we might give our master loyalty: our family, our tribe, our lodge, our union, our school, our neighborhood, our city, our county, our nation. Superficial reflection reveals that most people do indeed place the nation above the others; for example, most parents will yield their sons to the nation's military demands, even though their death might ensue, mirroring to the world thereby that loyalty to their nation comes before loyalty to their family.

Amongst the bad news we daily suffer is that of urban rot. The cities are in trouble. The culprit most responsible for the decline of our cities is the United States; its demands have drained our energies from city affairs and focused our vision on marble Washington. Our civic pride has turned to tasteless ash while we have savored the sweet taste of rising national power. That same culprit, to fend off our righteous anger, established a department for urban affairs, in an attempt to buy our silence. That federal department has been totally ineffective. Periodically, the newspapers print mayors' repeated complaints against the federal government. Among them are that a federal farm policy has "disinherited millions of farm families, driving masses of them into already crowded cities;" that a federal housing policy has "contributed to urban sprawl;" that a federal highway policy has "stimulated the suburban exodus;" that federal fiscal policies have been "inflationary and increased costs beyond the power of cities to meet them;" and that the federal government has cornered the most lucrative tax source, the income tax, while cities are restricted to tax sources that are increasingly resented and are further hedged by state policies that limit their taxing and borrowing power.

Beyond the postal system and federal office payrolls, the federal government does not send cities back a constructive, decent amount of their tax money. Much of what does return is as welcome as a kick to the groin. Destructive freeways, cement, medium-security asylums called public housing, and neighborhood-busting redevelopment schemes are a cursed state and federal legacy, and so are "defense" industries whose federal largess does nothing to improve or enhance the life conditions of city inhabitants.

Severance from federal and state governments would yield cities a bulging treasury. If instead of sending our business, corporation, and income tax monies out of the city, we were to retain them, the opportunity for civic improvement would be so immense that it momentarily stuns the mind and the imagination. But only momentarily. This tract is my attempt to rouse your civic imagination from its deep nationalistic slumber. Entertain for a moment my monstrous thesis; cast off for a moment your red-white-and-blue fig leaf, reverse time and the Fall, and return with me to a recoverable Eden where we may concinnate comfortably, money swelling our coffers, having freed our cities from the federal bandit.

To discomfit the persistent nation-lover, I have saved until last the most powerful reason of all: Only by returning to the city-state can we recover philosophy.

Philosophy does not thrive on a diet of printed words; it lives in spoken discourse; it is goaded into existence by conflict and contradiction and is nurtured by adversaries who stay to talk, and talk, and talk. Americans are seldom adept enough at conversation to sweep their talk to a philosophical level. What chiefly interests them is gossip, banter, sports, and deals. They have little patience for extended, rational discourse, for discourse which comes to an end either when the parties are exhausted or when they reach consensus.

The American substitute for philosophical talk is legislation: let the legislator put another law on the books to resolve social conflict, and the rest of us should get on with business. Too many Americans are content to fondle the illusion of political participation by playing their sixty-second act in the theatre of the polling booth.

"Yes," you might say, "but we cannot all get into the big show; at least high discourse is heard among those we elect to the capitols and city halls."

No one who has followed legislation, who has testified, who has observed the circus of investigating committees, who has tried to engage his representatives in meaningful public discussion would say that. True enough, officials listen to public testimony; but you cannot question them at hearings, you cannot engage them as they swivel in high-backed, leather chairs on lofty platforms, gazing down on us from behind their bored masks.

"Yes," you say, "but that is for august, public show to preserve the dignity of and to elicit respect for their office. It is open to everyone to lobby his representatives, to go to their offices, to speak personally with them."

This reply has some limited truth. There are supervisors and legislators who are available for extended talk, though even they are hampered by the forms to which their fellow legislators cling in order to keep the populace at a safe distance.

I do not intend my criticism of Americans' excessive reliance on legislation to be a criticism of their personal inadequacy to conduct extended, high philosophical conversation; nor do I intend my criticism of legislators' attachment to self-protective, insulating forms to be a personal criticism of them. All of us are victims. We are victims of governmental elephantiasis; our governments are too large to be governed in any other way than by distant, harried representatives, all, that is, except our cities. Our mayors and city supervisors, after all, walk amongst us, sleep and eat amongst us, and carry on their duties on home soil; they are, in short, our neighbors.

By returning to the city-state, cities can be freed from the condition that numbs the tongue of philosophy and sanctions the remoteness of a government from its people.

Consider how it is with philosophy, now. Philosophy has been scholasticized; it is confined to college and university classrooms, and even in the schools it is confined to a few students and professors. Philosophy has been jargonized; terms and distinctions that once flourished in native argument have been transplanted to the coolhouse of philosophic systems. "Demonstrate," "certain," "free," "justify," "argument," "real," "rules," "judgment," "proposition," "sense," "analyze," "persuade," "commend," "rational," "contingent," "explanation," "ascribe" are examples of terms that figure prominently in contemporary philosophical discourse; few of the ways that philosophers use those terms will be familiar to the "layman." These esoteric uses serve only the professional philosopher because he has purposes which he no longer shares with the "layman."

Men in intellectual conflict who reason together over a period of time find they need to make distinctions and must use them carefully. Terms such as those I mentioned were generated and used in the heat of argument; and the heat of argument brings the blush of life to their cheeks; they are seen by the contenders to be as necessary to their dialectic as chess pieces are to chess players. Philosophers tend to concentrate on distinctions and continually refine them. This is the natural outcome of sustained intellectual conflict, but professional philosophers all too often lose their touch with public life; the relevance of their distinctions then ceases to be common knowledge and philosophy's lifeline to the people and their affairs—the very womb of those distinctions—is cutlassed cleanly through.

An immediate example of this relation between life, conflict, and distinctions lies on the mirror of a little self-reflection. Someone in mild or violent disagreement with my thesis might well characterize these pages as a blatant attempt to persuade the unwary reader, while the reader who agrees with me may reply that the presence of rational arguments shows an honest attempt to demonstrate the thesis. The disagreement between two such parties really cannot profitably proceed much further without discussion of the distinction between *persuasion* and *demonstration* and without some clarification of the notion of *argument*. Such a discussion carried on with sophistication would be philosophy. Those three italicized terms are among the terms I listed as central to contemporary philosophic discourse, but their importance and their point is lost without hooking them back onto the partisan passions which they arm.

Philosophy cannot be restored to the people except under favorable circumstances. That requires a social unit of optimum size. This means a place *small* enough for high discourse to have an effect, and *large* enough to engage the full scope of man's capabilities and interests. Major cities have optimal philosophical size. They have a population large enough to support the full diversity of our society and are blessed with a compactness which makes citizens easily accessible to one another. Some, perhaps, are too large and themselves need to be divided into smaller cities.

Were governmental leaders, longshoremen, business men, artists, intellectuals, philosophers, professional men, laborers, actors, students, secretaries, labor leaders, journalists, ministers, tradesmen, musicians, clubwomen, clerks, salesmen, housewives, journeymen, teachers and professors, waiters, retirees, junior leaguers, social workers, and patrons to try to restore philosophy to our cities, they could find each other easily accessible were they to agree to meet for extended, purposeful, high conversation in restaurants, bars, and coffee houses. Philosophically responsible talk in your city could make a difference to what happens there; it can make little difference to what happens in your state or in the United States. State and national communication must rely on books, magazines, radio, and television, all primarily one-way media.

Philosophy, however, is dialogue, a two-way exchange; it is challenge and response; proposal and agreement; suggestion and amplification; claim and refutation. Philosophy is public reasoning; its natural habitat is the city; it is communeication. Philosophy is too precious to be the sole possession of professional philosophers; it is too dependent on passionate conflict to be confined to the printed page. Imprisoned philosophy becomes scholasticized.

Inhabitants of cities, concentrate your thoughts, your energies, your loyalty, your money, your spirit, your talk on your city. Most of what you do you do in your city. What you do in your state and in the United States is done in them only because your city is physically located in them. States and the United States lead deputized, parasitical lives. Let your acts be city, and only city, acts.

The restoration of philosophy to your city, an ample treasury, decent (free of federal tax) prices on wines and spirits, and peace are powerful inducements to rally our fellow inhabitants around an independence movement. If you are convinced of the advantages of independence but do not have the heart to face the legal and practical difficulties of attaining independence, let me say this to you: At least allow the vision of a free city to feed and increase your loyalty to your captive city; all will not be lost if your perspective of your city has been sufficiently tilted by my proposal to start you thinking afresh about what your city can become. That your city is presently in state and federal bondage does not lessen your responsibility to make the best of what you have. Nor does it lessen because you entertain little hope that it will be free in the near future.

Let me remind you that the original form of our polity has been castrated. Once cities and states were important social units that stood between family and nation. Their elimination as centers of power has left a gap that extends all the way from the family to the nation. Further, the family has been reduced to an immediate family—parents and children—that plays a diminishing role in many lives; and even that role is threatened by a rising divorce rate. The gap is widening; if it proceeds unchecked, it will extend until there is nothing between the individual and the nation. This is national totalitarianism with a vengeance.

To denture this social gap, our citizens typically have joined organizations and institutions. But these social units are not fit substitutes for cities, for, instead of being responsible for all aspects of human life under the standard of the common good of its members, they either cater to the special goods of some members of the whole—as does Rotary International or a labor union or a youth club—or they supply the needs of some one aspect of human life as does a church or a sports club. A good example of this was reported recently, by a New York resident. "All of my life," he said, "I've wanted to feel a belonging, a sense of community, a brotherhood, and there's nothing in one's work or this crazy urban world you can get it from." Then he reports getting it from a "Men's Liberation" group that's not "just rapping about politics or baseball scores; we're talking about feelings."

Though you may not feel ready to join a City Liberation Front, at least you ought to join a movement to restore some power to the cities, a half-way measure that is more welcome than the void in which we now soundlessly, crazily tumble as unheeded civic orphans.

Given that our loyalty, attention, money, energy, and intelligence have been devoted primarily to our nation rather than to our cities, we are not surprised that cities have suffered from our neglect. They have, in fact, suffered mortal blows. We no longer have cities. We have populated site fragments located in a region christened with a city name. Our city sites are occupied by fragments—they are a Many that must be unified into a One before these fragments can function as a city-site for the good life. In the next chapter, I explain the ancient philosophical issue of the One and the Many and relate it to our fragmented, so-called cities.

4 THE ONE AND THE MANY

Here are luvly phraggmentes that tugg
laevishe pytie frum mye harte.
— FANEBIUS PERLYNG

The unity of a city is a prized and hard-won achievement which does not come automatically with its charter. A philosophical task facing city dwellers is the identification of a principle of unity for a city's essential parts, its neighborhoods. Until civic unity is achieved, our cities will continue to be the battlefield for the War of the Neighborhoods.

❦ ❦ ❦

HOW DESPERATELY WE sometimes care about unity! How troubled we are to find our favorite photograph of our favorite person torn asunder; to hear of a man and wife, once close in marriage, now separated and the marriage destroyed; to read of a country ripped by revolution.

How annoyed we sometimes are to suffer the loss of unity. A hammer's head flying off the handle in mid-construction; the pages of a book missing just when we are about to get a crucial clue; a candle without a wick at a seduction dinner.

Things which may be torn, ripped, separated, dissolved, destroyed, broken, shredded, dismantled, unhinged, loosened, smashed, splintered, crushed, severed, crumbled, or disrupted are things which have a unity; they are also complex; they have a unity despite their complexity; they hold their several parts together so they count as One thing though they have Many parts.

CONCERNING THE TASSELED HAMMER

How is it that Many things can become One thing?

That is easy to answer. The Many become parts of the One.

I see lying before me a handle, a hammer head, and a tassel. How may each of them become a part?

Anything may become a part by being attached to something else, those things then forming a new thing. By attaching the handle to the hammer head, a new thing, the hammer, is made. And if instead of attaching the handle to the hammer head, we attached the tassel to the handle, the tassel and the handle would become parts; they would become parts of the new thing, the tasselhandle. We could also by the same method have a tasselhead and a tasselhammer.

Things don't become parts by being attached to other things, and I've got two arguments to prove it. The first argument is this: A thing may be a part without being attached; this is shown by the fact that we think a handle is a hammer part even if it's not attached to the hammer head, and that we believe an automobile parts depot is filled with auto parts even though they aren't attached to autos. The second argument is this: There are wholes whose parts aren't literally attached to each other as hammer parts are. For example, the notes of a piece of music aren't attached, nor are husband and wife always attached, nor are members of a club literally attached to each other.

REGARDING POTENT PARTS

Whoa! One argument at a time. Let me handle the first one first. It's true that some things may be parts although not attached, such as the auto parts. In that case they're potential parts. They become actual parts when they are attached; the attachment transforms the Many parts into a One.

How can you tell that something is a potential part?

By seeing that it can perform the same function as an actual part. A piston in the parts bin is an engine part because it can perform the same function as the piston in the engine.

You're in trouble, fella'. What are you going to say about the first piston ever made, before it was attached to other engine parts? It can't be a potential part according to your view because there does not yet exist another actual part whose function it could perform. You've made the actual part parent to the potential part. It should be the other way around.

I think you're absolutely right. We have the concept of an engine and its parts before we have the actual engine and its parts. We conceive a piston as a potential part because we understand the function, the role, that it would play were it to become a part of an actual engine. Conception doesn't require the existence of an actual engine.

So now you say that you can tell that something is a potential part if you can conceive that it would perform a function in some whole.

Yes. And the One and the Many must be conceived together, for a thing cannot be conceived as a part unless it is conceived as the part of some whole, and a thing can't be conceived as a whole unless it is conceived as consisting of functioning parts. To conceive of the One is to conceive of the Many in functioning relationships.

OBSCENE INCIDENTS

Since you changed your views about potential parts, would you care to change your views about actual parts?

Do you think I should?

Yes, I do. You said that a thing is an actual part if it is attached to another part. But you made it a requirement for a potential part that it be conceived to perform some function were it to be attached. Shouldn't you require that actual parts also perform a function? Take a tassel, for example. Do you think a functionless tassel is an actual part of a hammer just because it's attached to the hammer?

I believe that the tassel is an actual part of the hammer, but I don't believe it is a hammer part.

How can you deny it's a hammer part if it's actually attached to the hammer?

Make like a philosopher. Make another distinction. Some things which are attached to other things to make a whole are essential and others are incidental. Not all parts which are actually attached are essential; some attached parts are incidental. Only the handle and the head are hammer parts because they are the only parts which are essential. The tassel is not a hammer part because it's incidental, not essential.

How can we tell which attached parts are essential?

They're the ones that perform a function without which the whole couldn't fulfill its purpose. A wick is essential to a candle if the candle is to give light. A piston is essential to an engine if the engine is to produce power. The tassel doesn't contribute to the hammer's capacity to drive or pull nails, so it's incidental.

I take it that a thing may be essential to one whole and incidental to another?

Exactly. Obscene words are essential to obscene phone calls but incidental to prayers.

ATTACKING ATTACHING

Now that you mention phone calls and prayers, I'm reminded of my second argument against an attachment theory of the One, namely, that there are some wholes whose unity isn't accounted for by saying that their parts are literally attached to each other. The words in phone calls aren't literally attached to each other, nor are the notes in a symphony, nor are the neighborhoods of a city, nor are the persons who are party to a friendship; in none of these cases are the Many physically attached to each other; yet in each instance we have a One—a phone call, a piece of music, a city, and a friendship.

I think you're absolutely right. I have been over-attached to using attachment as an explanation of how the essential Many can become a One because I've been thinking too exclusively about the unity of inert physical wholes. Your examples of a phone call, a symphony, friendship, and the city made me realize that. I'll have to think of a more general theory to account for the unity of different kinds of things.

❋ ❋ ❋

In thinking about unity, then, we have to keep several things in mind. First, we must remember that there are potential as well as actual parts. Secondly, that, because men are capable of conceiving and imagining, potential parts and wholes are independent of and may precede actual parts and wholes; man is not hedged in by actual existence but may transcend his existential circumstances. Thirdly, there is a difference between essential and incidental parts, essential parts being identifiable as those whose function is necessary if the whole of which they are a part is to fulfill its purpose. And, finally, we must remember that attachment is not the only relationship between the Many which unifies them into a One, for attachment, except in a metaphorical sense, applies only to some physical unities such as hammers and engines and not to such things as poems and songs.

If your city is to become a city-state, it is imperative that we begin to think seriously about The City. We must develop a conception of the city's purpose or function; given that function, we can identify the function that its potential parts must perform, and separate its essential from its incidental parts; after that, we can posit the relation(s) we want to establish between the Many essential parts in order that they be united into One functioning city.

It will help us to think through this philosophical assignment if we review Plato's solution to a similar one. His *The Republic* is the most philosophically satisfying response to a demand for civic unity; although I do not think that his solution can be ours, nevertheless, the angle of his attack on the problem will be clarifying.

For Plato, the function of a state is to provide for the well-being of its citizens. To accomplish this, Plato believes it needs three essential parts, each with a distinct function; which he identifies as three classes of persons: Artisans, auxiliaries, and rulers. The artisans perform the functions of producing and distributing both necessary and luxury goods; the auxiliaries are the soldiers; and the rulers are the members of the government.

Plato's ideal rulers are philosopher-kings. This does not mean that philosophers should be pressed into thrones and crowned at hasty coronation rites but that, beginning with their youth, persons suited to be rulers must be molded into philosophers to equip them for their function—the establishment and preservation of a just state. A state, for Plato, is just and, thus, can perform its function, if its parts are coordinated. This coordination is the responsibility of the rulers; it is accomplished when each of the city's three parts performs the function for which its members are best suited and each is prevented from performing the function of another part. This coordination of different parts is analogous to the coordination of different players in baseball; if the players coordinate, they are unified into a team; lack of coordination produces chaos. The unifying relationship among the essential parts of a city-state, according to Plato, is complementary coordination. He pointed out to fellow Athenians that they had a large stake in a unified state: With unification, the state is just; without unification, it is unjust. A prudent citizen will be interested in working for unification to the degree that he is interested in living in a just state, one consideration being that a just state will do more for his well-being than an unjust one will do.

Plato recognized that the Greek city-states, as he knew them, had become more complex, the arts more specialized, and the citizens more distant from the rulers than the feudal societies depicted in traditional Greek literature. The *Iliad* presented a hero-ethics. Powerful, giant nobles cleaving their way through the flesh of barbarians, setting courageous examples for imitation, and returning after victory to their rural strongholds loaded with the spoils of war became anachronistic figures in a sophisticated city-state. In Athens such nobles were no longer the central moral feature; the Greek cultural landscape had changed.

Plato saw that his task was to bring Greek thought and literature into touch with the contemporary moral realities. To do this required replacing a hero-ethics with a city-ethics. The ethical responsibilities in urban centers had become too diverse and too many to be personally supervised by a single nobleman. Such individual supervision had been feasible in quiet pastoral fiefs but was no longer possible in a bustling commercial metropolis. If the work in cities was to get done, moral responsibility had to be internalized into each citizen. In a hero-ethics only the hero-noble internalizes his responsibility; all the others are like errant children who do their duty only if the towering noble himself hovers over them. Except for the hero himself, it is an ethics imposed by external authority.

Plato's major effort in *The Republic* was directed to showing his fellow citizens that there is an internal sanction against being an unjust man, a sanction which operates even though the unjust acts you perform are undetected by external agents, noble or otherwise. The unjust man reaps a rotten, unhealthy soul.

The sweep of Christianity in the West has brought with it enough emphasis on guilt and conscience to have made Plato's conclusion about the civic need for the internalization of responsibility familiar to us. We don't always assume our responsibility, but at least we're fully aware that we ought to internalize our ethics. But our primary civic problem is different from Plato's because the problems that faced the Greek city-states are different from those that face our cities.

Our problem is the loss of community with the consequent pathology that I outlined in Chapter 2—alienation, isolation, social ineffectiveness and aimlessness, truncated benevolence and excessive self-centeredness, insecurity, inability to will uninhibited commitment, moral confusion, ungrounded suspicions and fears, and shame at our reluctant withdrawal from civic existence. Our drive for unity must aim at producing community. Plato did not have to worry about community; we do. The parts that Plato had to unify were the producers, soldiers, and rulers that had sprung into increased prominence, and conflict, with the rise of large, commercial Greek cities. They were the Many he had to unify into One. Since we have a different problematic, the city-state must perform a different function for us than it did for him, and, consequently, the essential parts of a city will be different for us, as will their functions.

The reach for community has been persistent and varied. The homey little suburban tract of a manageable size with a communal swimming pool and recreation hall is an attempt to form village-islands in a swirling, vasty deep. Young people form gangs to roam the chartless city jungle as pirates once roamed the seas. Hippies, desperate for human warmth, despising suburbia, disapproving of gangs, and rejected by the city, have revived communes and the tribe in city and out. Ethnic minorities are reviving and celebrating the culture of their ancestral home in answer to the ghetto walls erected between them and other parts of the city by prejudice and segregation. These attempts at community do not solve our problem; they either fail outright, or exacerbate the problem, or are partial, or are utopian.

The problem is obviously still before us. At this point, I remind you of the flow-chart and my explanation of it (page 19ff), and relate them to the ideas of this chapter. In this essay I will claim: that the *potential parts* of a city are its neighborhoods; that they are its *essential parts* because they perform a *function* necessary to the functioning of a city, the function of the neighborhoods being to provide access to moral power (Chapter 10); that citizens' exercise of moral power establishes the relation of understanding between neighborhoods, which is the *unifying relation between parts*; that, upon the city being unified, it can perform the *function of the whole*, which is to create unified, realized persons.

Before closing out our background discussion of the One and Many issue, we should consider and evaluate some theories about social unity that have been proposed previously. This is the subject of the next chapter.

5 SOME OVER-THE-HILL UNITIES AND THE DEATH OF PERSON

T'is filausofers what bedde
daun wyth paradoxyes.
  —FANEBIUS PERLYNG

The next two chapters are a negative prelude to my positive theory about the nature of man and society. In this chapter, I plow under a rich growth of untenable theories about the unity of society. This will prepare the soil for my thesis about civic unity. Among the theories about the unity of society that I turn under are chain, wheel, team, organism, person, sub-society, and contract theories.

❁ ❁ ❁

IN THE LAST chapter we saw that it is important but not obvious how we are to weld the Many into One, how we are to achieve social unity. If we do not know social unity's nature, our efforts to achieve it will be as the gropings of a blind man in a soundless, unfamiliar territory. Divination of the nature of social unity has always been central to the efforts of social and political philosophers, as it must now be for us if we are to rationally and deliberately set about forging the unity of our divided cities.

The question we face here is this: What relations must hold

between Many social parts if they are to be unified into One social whole?

We are searching for unifying relations among social parts that will play a role analogous to that which functional attachment plays for physical objects and their parts. In thinking about society, philosophers generally have sought for the unifying relations by reflecting on analogies. They compare societies to such things as contractual arrangements, chains, wheels, and teams whose principle of unity they believe they understand; since society is analogous—similar—to those things, society's principle of unity must be similar; hence, the similarity leads them, they believe, to understand society's unity.

We must beware of exclusive reliance on the use of analogies. This becomes clear when we find that society has been compared to a lot of different things whose principles of unity are actually quite dissimilar. Which analogy is the "true" source of understanding? Clearly, one can't determine that from the analogies alone; they lead to contrary answers; one must know something about society that doesn't come from the analogies alone in order to know which comparison is the informative one.

Yet I do not wish to choose one analogy over another just because a given society resembles one of the analogues, for example, a chain. What I am after is a conception of an ideally unified society. I want to know what a city *ought* to be like and that is frequently different from what it is *actually* like. In the discussion of potential and essential parts in the last chapter, we saw that the conception of a whole and its parts may precede the actual whole and its parts. This holds true for the city and its parts also. My choice of analogy will be governed by my conception of an ideal city that it is within our reach to achieve.

What I am looking for in the way of an analogy should yield a model of societal relations that will give us community without conformity; individuality, not eccentricity; cooperative autonomy instead of control; diversity without physical conflict; and civic commitment that stops short of patriotism.

But what of the traditional analogies? A city may have the unity characteristic of a chain. If we compare inhabitants to links, and the overlapping involvement of two individuals to the interlocking of two links, then, since we can trace a chain between any two remote individuals by tracing a series of intermediate overlaps, most cities have a chain-like unity. Someone that you know, P_1, knows somebody, P_2, who knows somebody, P_3, who knows somebody, P_4, who knows the Mayor. So does that make you know the Mayor? Clearly the unity of a chain is unsatisfactory for a city because it permits a remoteness of parts which makes us strangers to a sense of community.

The analogy of the wheel with its spokes converging to a common hub overcomes the remoteness of the chain's parts. The wheel, though, is not an acceptable analogy for most persons who have matured under American political ideals; identifying the government with the central hub implies too much central control over the lives of citizens, and tends to make the good of the government primary and the good of the individual citizen secondary. Spokes do not have the autonomy we desire for persons. Moreover, the structure of the wheel is too simple to be a useful model for our contemporary cities, since it provides no analogues for the sub-societies that are a feature of our complex urban society. A wheel might be a satisfactory analogy for a tribe but not for a modern city.

I have already indicated one reason for rejecting the team analogy in my discussion of Plato's theory, namely, that while the team analogy fitted Plato's ends because he had to emphasize the responsible role each citizen had to assume if an increasingly complex society were to provide the services demanded by citizens, it does not fit ours because our cities' pressing problems are not concerned with the coordination of roles. Once people get jobs, they do not need to worry about the coordination of their efforts with those of others. Our society is resplendent with managerial brass and braid. But even if this were not the case, Plato's analogy would still not be advisable for our cities because his stress on the coordination of team roles places too much emphasis on the person as a functional entity. Being a carpenter, or a rate clerk, or an attorney, or a teacher, or a supervisor, or a salesman doesn't exhaust our lives. There is much more to a person than is dreamed of in Plato's assignation of civic roles. We expect society to create persons possessing something additional to their civic functional talents. A historical manifestation of this expectation is the liberal arts college whose purpose is not merely to train persons for a job but to equip them for a satisfying life outside their job as well.

Team spirit, in Plato's sense, does contain something of the sense of community that we desire, but, based as it is on function alone, it is too narrowly conceived.

The animal organism is one of the most persistently popular and persuasive analogies used in explaining how persons are bound into a social unity; it is used also to persuade us that the relations between persons and society are similar to those between the parts and the whole organism. Its popularity and persuasiveness probably depend on two obvious features we can all observe about our own bodies. First, the well-being, nay, the very existence, of the whole organism depends heavily on the balanced functioning of at least some parts; as goes the liver, for example, so goes the life of the whole. Life is the sign of unity and unity is achieved by mutually supportive functioning of the parts; similarly, the "life" of society depends on mutually supportive persons. Secondly, once a part is cut off from the organism, that part ceases to be a functioning, living entity. Thus, a severed hand goes into the discard or becomes a grisly reminder to the morbid types who preserve their departed hand in a clear, alcohol-filled jar. The poor devil cut off from the social whole suffers the same fate as the severed hand, or if never brought up in a social whole, never becomes a person at all.

The organism analogy has been popular also because some thinkers find it is well suited for justifying a tightly organized society and for pressing on individuals an overwhelming sense of gratitude to the state without which they could have no significant existence. On this broad plane of gratitude, they can lay a heavy demand for obedience to the state.

But if potato tubers could feel, they wouldn't have the same sense of gratitude nor the same devotion to the whole as you would were you to make the animal organism analogy your guide to social unity. Although potato plants are organisms, their tubers don't fall into immediate decline upon separation from their parent plant. The tubers sprout, and if planted, flourish into plants. The organism analogy cannot be used to put the screws to you unless a particular kind of organism and a particular kind of part is spotlighted.

The organism analogy cannot be used unreflectively, then; you must pick the kind of organism you wish to analogize from, because different kinds of organisms lend themselves to different analogical uses. Pretty clearly, most organism theorists have animals in mind, and frequently human animals. Using human organisms gives the theorist a chance to enrich the analogy; he can, for example, compare a person's will to the executive function of government and his mind to the collective intelligence of legislative bodies. Through such elaboration of the organism analogy does this particular conception of the body politic grow.

However useful the organism and person analogies may be to people who are interested in theories of the state, they are less useful to those interested in a theory of society. The distinction between state and society is often obscured by those who use the organism and person analogies. To confuse the distinction between states and society is like confusing motor-cycles with a vehicle. A state is a particular instrument of so-ciety, as a motorcycle is a particular vehicle for man. To leave one state for another is not leaving society any more than switching from a motorcycle to a car is giving up vehicles.

The freedom to move from one state to another, to judge a state as wanting, to refuse to be loyal to a particular state are opportunities that we recognize are available and that we wish to preserve. Yet these are the kinds of things organism theorists typically wish to deny us; they want to bind us to a particular state as an animal part is bound to the whole.

Without being a part of some society or another, we would never have become persons, but once made persons, we do not have the restrictions on us that parts of animal organisms nor-mally do. My search is for an analogy that will help convey the kind of relations that must exist in a unified society if per-sons are to be continuously created by that society. I am not searching for an analogy that will extract a puling patriotism.

Yet another analogy that I find inadequate is the sub-society analogy. People who think of the unity of a society on lines suggested by sub-societies think that the principle of unity for societies is or should be the same as that for sub-societies, namely, that all the members do or should share a common purpose or goal.

That members of sub-societies should share purposes is not surprising. The very reason for forming a sub-society is to fos-ter goals already held in common. That is why we have the American Philosophical Society or the Realty Association. To demand this kind of unity of societies, however, is asking them to go on the equivalent of a war-time footing; a garrison state demands dedication to a common goal, but it isn't ex-actly my idea of an ideal society.

I won't deny that members of society share very general goals—for example, that their society should create richly endowed persons—but this generality allows the co-existence of different, specific goals not all of which need to be shared by all members of that society.

The last analogy I plow under is probably the most popular, persistent, and, I believe, the most pernicious one. That is the contract theory, which is often claimed to be an account of the origin as well as the unity of society.

The contract theory asserts that social units are unified by virtue of a contract that individual persons make with each other. Those who hold a contract theory often try to account for the existence of the agreement by stating that the individuals who are parties to the contract realized that united they would win benefits that they could not win as isolated individuals, including the vital benefit of self-preservation.

The contract theory of unity suggests a theory of social genesis more obviously than the other analogies we've considered. The signing of a partnership contract, for example, not only binds the partners into a unity but is simultaneously the very birth moment of the partnership.

On the supposition that society's genesis is similar to a partnership's, we have to assume that there was no society until a contractual agreement existed. This means that prior to the agreement, the individuals who were party to the agreement had to exist in a "state of nature." They would, as "natural" beings existing prior to society, be like animals, without a language, without morality, and without social wit. The contract theory's plausibility, however, requires that the "natural" individuals who were party to the original contract would be just like those persons born into and reared in the post-contract society. This is pernicious doctrine because it leads people to be more cavalier about the importance of society than they should or would be if they realized that it is through society that we are the artisans, the creators, of persons. It is also nonsensical doctrine, for only those born into a society have the advantage of inheriting existing languages, morality, and socially shared knowledge denied the "natural" beings.

Despite the absurdity of supposing that there could be persons without a society, the contract theory has had an extraordinary appeal to Westerners. Part of the explanation for this popular appeal is that the chief stabilizing factor among people in a suspicious, clawing, mercantile society is the contract. Hour after hour, most people's daytime activities are governed by explicit or implicit contracts. To narrow minds occupied almost exclusively with business, contracts seem central to the entire human flow.

Another partial explanation for the persistence of the contract theory can be traced to a confusion in the contract theorist's mind between sub-societies and society, and, as in the organism theory, between states and society. Persons in society do indeed often voluntarily band together to form sub-societies and states. You almost certainly have banded, joined, or vowed. Persons have by agreement started or joined states, trade unions, corporations, orchestras, co-operatives, marriages, social clubs, service organizations, and schools. But these social units aren't society. They are sub-societies catering to and supportive of special interests developed by society.

Mistaking the origin of sub-societies for the origin of society inflates the illusion that persons exist prior to and independently of societies just as they exist prior to and independently of the formation of sub-societies. Unless you hold the pennant of difference between society and sub-societies steadily before you, you will be insensitive to and unappreciative of the person-creating role of society. This difference is important, too, in thinking about the city. If the city is to be more than a sub-society, it must accept the obligation of creating persons.

Another part of the explanation of the contract theory's popularity lies in a deeper, less accessible region. The skin of America's morals is tattooed with rugged "individualism."

Rugged individualism displays garish self-reliance and independence, which lead persons to suppose that their existence as humans and their self-realization is prior to and independent of society's existence and realization. This order of events is precisely the one suggested by the contract theory—a group comes into existence and its nature is determined because prior existing and determining persons contractually agree to bring the group into existence. However, beneath the tattooed surface lies the deeper reality of the civic alienation of our citizens from each other and from their society. This is the deeper source of the contract theory's popularity, because while rugged individualism seduces us into accepting the contract theory, rugged individualism itself is widely accepted because it is a defense mechanism against widespread alienation.

Alienation from society and others occurs because society fails to fulfill its obligation to create persons; alienation occurs when the society no longer affords persons opportunities for self-realization. The shock of alienation registers in the human consciousness during naked moments of wretched, lonely self-appraisal. Seldom recognized for what it is, alienation is usually mistakenly interpreted as personal inadequacy to fulfill the dream of life. We are weakest while nostalgic; it is at such times—when caught looking backward to the latter end of our school years or to the first jig of pleasure at earning our own money at a job, before being whitened by the bleach of profit—that we lay ourselves against the ruler of our youth's ambition, a ruler lovingly standardized by American dream-merchants, and find ourselves to be runted subordinates in a society where life's promises are cashed in only by princes of position, power, influence, money, notoriety, or fame.

Alienation forces withdrawal into the self. The alienated person is thrown on his own resources because he finds none offered him by society. In self-defense, he is driven to imagine himself as a self-sufficient, self-contained atom of existence. This emphasis on the rugged, independent self lends the contract theory of society a specious plausibility because it leads us, the alienated, to believe we are fully realized persons prior to the creation (and re-creation) of society and to ignore society's role in the creation of persons. As I indicated earlier in my discussion of the city-state as end–functional (Chapter 2, page 20f), unified, realized persons and unified, realized societies come into existence simultaneously; neither precedes the other. This is a logical necessity as my analysis of the concept of person in Chapter 7 will show, and refutes the contract theory of social unity.

Uncomfortably many Americans have bought rugged individualism. If one motive for doing so is because it is a defense mechanism against alienation as I have argued, the prevalence of this doctrine in America is a devastating reflection of the massive failure of our society to support persons' on-going, creative self-realization. I think that the oft-remarked-on fact that Americans are "joiners" also shows that our society has failed to help citizens realize themselves. Joining something or other is felt to be necessary because cities have failed to satisfy their social hungers. "Joining" is a compromise defense against our civic alienation. To avoid complete alienation and a subsequent reduction to Robinson-Crusoehood, part-persons flee to part-societies; they seek refuge in and identification with sub-societies.

The subject is roses. "In deepest sympathy on the death of Person" it says on the rose wreath. Let us draw closer so we can hear the funeral oration.

My remarks are not intended for the mourning survivors alone. They are also intended for the deceased. I wish he were here. They tell me he's having a drink in the Glad Hand bar. Perhaps some one of you will be able to get his ear later. I hope so, for his sake.

Person died at midnight on Wednesday. I could tell. There was a change in him, even though he had long been in decline. Thursday morning when he got on the bus, he sat down beside me, never said a word, just stared out the window the way that makes you embarrassed because it makes you notice how the bus is jiggling everybody up and down. After a while I asked him if he felt all right. He said he hadn't slept well after midnight, but that wasn't it. Then he said, "What's the point of kidding myself. I'm not going to make it big."

The spark of life was gone. Person had joined the living dead. He had tied the value of his life exclusively to making it big. When the dream of achieving bigness vanished, sweet life flew out the window. Unfortunately, he has no more options; society isn't organized to offer him any other fulfillment than bigness. Poor Person.

Abandoned by society, dumbly aware of his inability to recreate himself, his outcast status calcifying into a rigid alienation, Person will soon regard society, which could have been his natural ally, as his legitimate prey, while apologists, responding to a desperate need, prescribe for Person the protective covering of a glorified "rugged individualism."

Not even a has-been because never a was, Person is dead now. We bid him farewell forever unless society in a newly found bounty makes it possible for Person to be re-born Amen.

In this chapter, I have tried to pry your belief loose from several familiar theories of social unity, ending with the contract theory. I consider it to be the most plausible and pervasively held theory because its strength comes from its tie to the doctrine of rugged individualism, which, in turn, draws its main sustenance from widespread alienation. Although the notion of rugged individualism is a social and moral doctrine, I believe that it is underwritten by a particular metaphysical doctrine about the self. This metaphysical view is what I explore in the next chapter.

I have laid heavy blame on alienation at several places in this essay. In the chapter after next, I sketch a relational theory of persons; it will give us a better insight into the nature of alienation, and, so, insight into the nature of its cure, which is the subject of the second chapter after the next. These are, of course, stones for the foundation of my own theory of social unity.

6 SUBSTANCE, APPEARANCE, AND INDIVIDUALISM

I am marryed tew apparentcy?
—FANEBIUS PERLYNG

Persons should not be thought of as if they were objects. To think of them as objects is pernicious because it generates an individualistic conception of man and thereby hinders the establishment of moral relations between persons. It is a metaphysical view of the self that leads to moral and social atomism.

❦ ❦ ❦

INDIVIDUALISM, I have said, is a defense mechanism employed when persons realize they have been abandoned by their society. That is its pitiful side. Individualism also encourages bravado, which is its rugged side. "Rugged" individualism is a clarion summons to gird up your muscles and to act vigorously to gain your goals; anyone caught hesitating to go roughshod in the world is spiked as a pallid, callow, sentimental bleedingheart; assertions of human interdependency are seen as admissions of weakness; competing is the great thing and the winner's reward is control over the losers; social welfare programs, medical aid, unemployment benefits, bankruptcy laws, and special help programs in the public schools are regarded as evidence of the victims' moral fiberlessness and failure rather than as evidence of a crippling social system; it is man heroically matching himself against a perpetually present, rugged frontier; self-interest is all; glory be to Daddy Warbucks!

Rugged individualism flies the proud banner of self-reliance and self-confidence. It also runs up the banner of freedom, of autonomy. In relying on and confiding in yourself alone, you can avoid buckling yourself to others. Any dependency relation you have with another person is unwelcome because it restricts your choices and actions, and, therefore, restricts your freedom. The other becomes as a millstone around your neck. In order to achieve maximum freedom—according to the ethics of rugged individualism—you should be the sole source of the energy required to achieve your goals. Human alliances are undertaken under the pressure of circumstances, and always reluctantly, because the acid of each alliance destroys a bit more of your freedom. It is assumed that human aid can be purchased only at the cost of freedom.

Given that the supreme value of rugged individualism is personal freedom, human relations are to be avoided except when you cannot accomplish your goals without help from others. The conditions which account for social relations, therefore, are those in which we look on other persons as means to our ends. The perfect relation to have with another person if we are absolutely forced to resort to using him as a means—according to individualism—is a one-way relation: You get help from him and he asks nothing in return, for, by asking for nothing, he does not restrict your freedom. The closest we come to this one-way relation between humans is in the master-slave relationship. The ideal logical outcome of rugged individualism when forced to operate in a world where we need others is slavery. The ideal outcome when persons are not forced to rely on the help of others is a "society" of personal atoms, each doing his own thing independently of others. This kind of society is essentially an aggregate of

atoms, since there are no mutual relations tying the atoms together; it is a Many that shuns Oneness. If we were to picture
an extreme form of alienation, we would picture the unrelated
aggregate of personal atoms which rugged individualism projects as its ideal.

Of course, the person committed to rugged individualism
does not want to be the slave of another because a slave suffers a minimum state of freedom. To avoid becoming another's
slave, a person must either have the power to be a master or
he must live in splendid isolation. Among a group of persons,
it is not logically possible for everyone to be a master; masters
cannot be masters without someone being a slave. Given that
no rugged individualist willingly becomes a slave, a power
struggle to determine who shall be masters and who slaves
is another logical outcome of rugged individualism. Might
doesn't make right, it makes Masters. To be caught in the toils
of the ethics of rugged individualism is to be caught permanently in the toils of war.

There is a way out of this permanent state of war that is
becoming more and more a practical possibility. With ad-
vances in technology, we can replace slaves with machines.
This makes possible the perfect one-way relationship because
machines help us accomplish our goals without asking for anything in return. Technology perfected would enable us to live
in complete freedom from others without struggle. The bliss
of living with machines would be chilled only by their lack
of love, respect, care, admiration, praise, encouragement, and
concern. This chill might be removed by programming the
machines to show by their behavior that they do love, respect,
care for, admire, praise, encourage, and are concerned for us.
Of course, our programming these human attitudes into the
machines would be the ultimate act of rugged individualism because they would, in effect, then be attitudes of self-
love, self-respect, self-care, self-admiration, self-praise, self-
encouragement, and self-concern.

The ethic of rugged individualism logically results, then, in alienation, slavery, war, and self-glorification. These results should be enough reason to reject it as our ideal ethical system. The fact that the results are exactly our present moral situation makes the philosophical task of fashioning an alternative more than an academic exercise.

I don't suppose anyone would willingly opt for rugged individualism if faced with these logical results. He might suicidally resign himself to this fate, however, if he thought that it was an unavoidable "human condition." Unfortunately, this seems to be exactly what many do think. I believe that most of our contemporaries are resigned to some form of the ethic of rugged individualism because they believe that the nature of persons leaves us with no alternative. I do not have in mind an appraisal of the moral nature of persons but, rather, a view of the metaphysical nature of persons. The metaphysical view of persons that underwrites rugged individualism is the view that a person is an object kind of thing called a substance.

I shall show how, in thinking that persons are substances, we are led to think of them as self-contained entities, atoms of existence, fundamentally isolated from each other because relations between them affect only the surface and not the core of each other's reality. In short, to think of persons as substances is to think of them as metaphysically alienated. This metaphysical alienation underwrites a form of moral and political alienation such as rugged individualism because it imposes a particular image of society on us. The image is that society is a collection of atoms, each atom being a person. Atoms are morally isolated from each other because moral and political relations between them fail to tie their core realities together into an integrated society; they tie only the surface appearance of persons together. This view of persons and their moral relations leaves us barren of any other than prudential reasons why we should treat others morally because nothing more profound than their appearance is at stake. Substance thinking makes a mystery of morality and of a commitment to social ideals.

We are like BB's scattered randomly on a plane; we touch only on the surface, if we touch at all.

Let us proceed to draw out what it is to think of a person as a substance, as, I suspect, you do.

The concept of substance is given its marching orders by our common sense notion of a physical object, so that to think of a person, a self, as a substance is to think of him on the model of a physical object. To be sure, not everyone who holds a substance theory of persons believes that the substance of persons is physical matter; they may hold that a person is a mental substance, a soul. Still, even as a mental substance, the person is thought of as a thing, an object, albeit a mental thing.

I have often noticed that at the mention of the word "metaphysics" or of metaphysical words such as "substance," people's eyes glaze over, they start acting slightly shifty, and you know they are wondering how they ever got themselves into such a situation. They are perfectly willing to leave metaphysics to the philosophers who apparently find some use for it, little knowing that they themselves are metaphysicians. People generally have too great a reverence and/or fear of Madame Metaphysics. Let us escort her from the study to the kitchen where we may comfortably consort with her.

A METAPHYSICAL INTERLUDE

The scene is Andrea and Homer's kitchen. They are engaged in their usual sort of after-dinner conversation.

ANDREA: I've been reading Descartes' *Meditations* again, Homer, and thinking about substance.

HOMER: That's swell, Andrea.

ANDREA: Why are your eyes glazing over?

HOMER: They always do that when you mention "substance."

ANDREA: You've simply got to get over that. You embarrass me in front of our friends.

HOMER: Can you help me?

ANDREA: I hope so. Look, Homer, suppose all your concepts were laid out before you. You'd find that they presented a cluster pattern. There would be a cluster of concepts that we use to think about economics, another we use to think about botany, another we use to think about food, another we use to think about law and so forth.

HOMER: I would?

ANDREA: Yes, and you would also notice that some concepts occur in every cluster. These concepts saturate all your thinking. You use them to think about anything. These pervasive concepts are metaphysical concepts.

HOMER: That doesn't sound complicated. Can you give me some examples?

ANDREA: Sure, and all of them perfectly familiar to you. Beginning and end, individual, character, unity, change, identity, and interaction. Oh, good, you're beginning to unglaze a little.

HOMER: And my breathing is getting more normal, too.

ANDREA: I think you're ready for substance.

HOMER: I'm starting to feel shifty, though.

ANDREA: Relax, dear, nothing could be simpler to explain. Substance is simply a concept you use in thinking, for example, about physical objects. You do think about physical objects, you know.

HOMER: Oh, yes, all the time, but I don't think I use substance all the time. Do I?

ANDREA: I think so. You think physical objects have a beginning and an end, don't you?

HOMER: Of course. Even the world has a beginning and an end.

ANDREA: Do you think things, or the world, are made out of nothing?

HOMER: You can't make something out of nothing. Even good fairies can't do that. The good fairy had to make Cinderella's horses out of mice and her carriage out of a pumpkin.

ANDREA: You agree with the first Greek philosophers, then. They thought there is a primary stuff out of which everything is made. Now listen to this: They called that primary stuff "substance."

HOMER: Am I unglazing just a little?

ANDREA: I think so. Now, Homer, you think that this substance is divisible because you think there are individual things.

HOMER: Absolutely. Here is an individual candle, there another one. And they are different individuals from the table they're sitting on. They're separate from each other.

ANDREA: Good. And don't you distinguish between a thing and its character? Don't you think that a character is something different from the thing that has the character?

HOMER: I suppose so, if you mean by a thing's character its properties or qualities.

ANDREA: That is what I mean. Roses are red, violets are blue. Now suppose that a thing's character were taken away from it. What would you have left? Suppose you take the taste, odor, color, shape, size, and so forth away from a piece of wax. What would you have left?

HOMER: I would have left whatever has those qualities.

ANDREA: Very clever. What should we call it?

HOMER: Substance?

ANDREA: Right. Substance and shadow, the thing and its appearance.

HOMER: Huh?

ANDREA: The character is the outward appearance, the show of the underlying reality which is substance. The character, the complex of qualities, inheres in the substance.

HOMER: What's this "inheres" bit? Is it as if the substance were some sticky stuff to which qualities stick, or what?

ANDREA: A visual and tactile metaphor won't do because even a "sticky stuff" is substance with a sticky character rather than "pure" substance. Substance is not something that can be observed by the senses; only its character appearance is sensible. Substance is the child of theory. It is an entity known only by reason. Descartes, in his *Second Meditation*, observes a piece of wax fresh from the beehive. When fresh from the hive it has a given character but, when he puts it by fire, it melts and changes its character completely. It tastes and smells different; it changes color and shape and size. Still we say it is the identical wax.

HOMER: I do. The wax didn't go out of existence just because its character changed.

ANDREA: Why do you suppose you can say it is the identical wax even though it has completely changed its character?

HOMER: Substance, again. The substance is the same before and after the wax melted; the substance did not go out of existence.

ANDREA: You see how marvelous you are at metaphysics, darling?

HOMER: Thanks. But I'm not yet wholly unglazed. I still don't understand how character inheres in substance.

ANDREA: There are some things you just have to accept. The mind must come to rest somewhere. Substance, being a child of reason, has whatever nature our mind needs in order to organize our experience of physical objects. For example, here is another use for substance. The character of an object is complex; it is made up of several qualities such as taste, smell, size, shape. Though the qualities are Many, the character is One. How is it possible that a character may have this unity?

HOMER: Like the good fairy, I utter a magic word: Substance! Since each of the characteristics inheres in the same substance, they are held together as a single character.

ANDREA: Excellent: More brandsey, please. Your eyes are getting quite unglazed now. Things change. Let me tell you how substance helps us unnerstand shange. A thing shanges when one of its qualities gets disinherited and nother inheres in ish playsh. Simple.

HOMER: Drunken qualities replace sober qualities.

ANDREA: That's because of the brandsey. One thing has an effect on another when they interact; it makesh a substance lose one characteristic and gain another.

HOMER: That makes me sad.

ANDREA: Poor Homer. Tell me all about it.

HOMER: You said a thing's character is only an appearance, an outward show. If interaction between things changes only the world's appearance but not its substance, reality never changes. Reality is static; it stays the same forever. That means our personal relations don't really change anything of our reality; we are doomed to affect only each other's appearance.

ANDREA: What a terribly sobering thought.

HOMER: You are beyond the hand of change even when it is the hand of someone who loves you very much. We are locked in our substances. There is an unbridgeable gulf between our substances. Our souls—

ANDREA: Souls?

HOMER: Yes, our souls. They are our substance, our reality. After all, I am not my body. Our souls are like BB shot lying on the plane of existence. Society amounts to no more than an aggregate of unconnected BB-souls. There is no true, profound interpenetration of one human substance by another.

ANDREA: But what makes you think . . .

HOMER: Andrea, I don't want you to ever read Descartes again. Look what his foul substance has done. Our personal character, sometimes so hard won, is vain foppery, the soul's dress, subject to fashion's whims, forever concealing our real, naked self from others. Do you realize what this means? I'll tell you. You may have the brains, but I've got the heart. What it means is that we are never able to reach beyond our own to another's reality. That means all our moral aspirations must sink to a base, rugged individualism or some similar stupid ethic, a kind of BB version of our moral condition. To a rugged individualist, only a featherbrained idealist could raise expectations for genuine relations and obligations between people.

ANDREA: But what makes you think . . .

HOMER: Don't stop me now. Thinking of humans as substances is merely a metaphysical version of human BB-hood; it is a metaphysical basis for yielding to belief in ultimate, unavoidable alienation; it is a metaphysical prop for a BB-ethic. According to your substance-cretins, we live a life of pretense if we think we can lay an obligation on somebody else because, in effect, our realities are sealed off from each other. As substances we are existentially independent; only our appearances are affected by human relations. Life is a series of transmigrations, which is just a series of transmogrifications of persons' appearance. In actuality, our hermetically sealed souls drift in eternal isolation, unperturbed, unruffled, unchanged, essentially uninvolved, shedding one appearance after another like a snake shucking last year's dead skin. Weep for them, Andrea. Weep.

ANDREA: Come, come, dear, the slough of despair doesn't suit you. We can escape this dreadful metaphysical fate. What makes you think that we have to think of persons as substances, as if they were like physical objects?

HOMER: You don't deny that we think of them that way, do you? After all, we do apply all the metaphysical concepts to humans that we apply to physical objects. Persons have beginnings and ends, birth and death; we distinguish one individual person from another; persons have character, personality; their character belongs to them and no one else, and may have a unity; persons change, the child and the adult are as different as the wax is before and after melting; persons main-

tain their identity even though their character changes completely; I remember a poem Bob Kennedy gave me, a Hindu
poem, he said:

> Death is only matter dressed
>   in some new form,
> A varied vest:
> From tenement to tenement
>   though tossed,
> The Soul does not change.
> Only the figure is lost!

And you won't deny that persons interact.

ANDREA: What is all that supposed to prove?

HOMER: That the metaphysical concepts—beginning and
end, individual, character, unity, change, identity, and interaction—apply to persons as well as to physical objects.

ANDREA: Just because they apply to persons doesn't by itself
prove that persons are substances. Substance happens to be
part of a particular metaphysical theory designed to explain
how metaphysical concepts apply to physical objects. But,
those concepts apply to every field. Remember?

HOMER: Sure, I remember. That's what makes them metaphysical concepts. So they do apply. So what, Brandy Andrea?

ANDREA: At least the glaze is gone, but you're still too damn
shifty, Homer. Those metaphysical concepts apply to economics. Take the idea of a market. Markets come and go; the
surrey market is kaput, dead. We distinguish the tobacco
market from the hair spray market. Markets have a character;
just read the *Wall Street Journal.* Markets have a unity; if they
didn't, we couldn't financially "grab" "the market"; there has
to be something you control when you control it. Markets
change; they rise and fall. And they have to have an identity
or we couldn't say the market has fallen. Today the market is
783; yesterday it was 785. One number is lower than the other;
but if the two numbers don't describe the same entity (it, the

market) at two different times, we couldn't say that *it* had fallen. Finally, markets interact; the auto market affects the steel market.

Here comes the big question, Homer. When you think of the market, do you think there is a substance that is its underlying reality?

HOMER: That's an easy one. No.

ANDREA: Well, there you are, we don't always need substance to explain how the metaphysical concepts apply. What makes you think we need it to explain how they apply to persons?

HOMER: To tell you the truth, I'm not sure.

ANDREA: The existence and nature of substance is entirely dependent on theory. It is a theoretical entity. We can keep it as long as it plays a necessary part in a good theory. But as soon as we reject the theory, we can reject substance. Substance becomes a useless piece of baggage that is best dropped. Don't you agree?

HOMER: I think I do. Some biologists once thought there was a life-force. They needed it to explain how "inert" matter could be alive, but now that we have more advanced chemical and physical theories to explain life, we don't need such an entity as "life-force" anymore. Good.

ANDREA: Do you think the substance theory of persons is a good one?

HOMER: You must not have taken my tirade seriously. Any metaphysical theory that leads to a bad ethic such as rugged individualism has got to be bad.

ANDREA: Why don't you throw it out, then?

HOMER: I don't know. Maybe I still think it's true.

ANDREA: You don't have to believe in the existence of substance in the way that you have to believe in the existence of candles. You can see, feel, smell, and taste candles, but you can't see, feel, smell, or taste substance. It's an entity invented by the mind to explain how we apply metaphysical concepts.

You admit you don't use it—so, you don't need it—to explain your talk about markets. Maybe the concept of a person is more like the concept of a market than it is like the concept of a physical object. If it is, then substance is a superfluous theoretical entity. Give up your old metaphysical habits; they only lead to rotten moral theories. You've got metaphysical freedom, sweetie. Reorganize your thought about persons.

HOMER: Freedom from substance! What a slogan! I like it. Do you mean we might think of a different theory of persons? I'd like one that makes a decent human society possible, a theory in which it is possible for human relations to affect the essence of each other's being. I'd like a theory that helps us understand how our very existence and nature are dependent upon the achievement of a set of moral relations to each other. We wouldn't have to live like BB's, then.

ANDREA: That's what I've always found dear in you, Homer, that streak of nobility, your hunger for moral dignity. It becomes you.

HOMER: Thanks, Andrea, but, tell me, what kind of a theory of persons would give us what I want, really?

ANDREA: You've been too generous with the brandy. I can't figure that one out tonight. It will just have to wait, Homer.

7 THE CREATION OF PERSONS

And Godde sayd, "Lett ther bee
rybs and realatyons."
— FANEBIUS PERLYNG

A person is a collection of relatents. His existence and his nature are dependent upon his relations to others. Since a person is by nature a relational being, man's social and communal nature receives a metaphysical foundation.

💮 💮 💮

BY EAVESDROPPING ON Andrea and Homer's conversation, we learned that we not only don't have to think of persons as substances, but that we don't want to think of them as substances because a substance theory of persons is a metaphysical version of alienation that supports the moral isolation of rugged individualism. With her comments on an economic market, Andrea taught us that we have the theoretical freedom to recast our metaphysical notion of a person. In this chapter, I take advantage of that freedom to suggest another theory of what a person is.

I recognize that though you may have seen intellectually that it is possible to escape from old metaphysical habits, and may indeed want to do so, yet it is no easier to drop your metaphysical habits than to drop your smoking or nail-biting habits. It may help you if we break some of the allied habits that reinforce your old metaphysical habits.

One allied habit brackets our notion of a person and his body. Once inside this buttery bracket you can easily slip from the thought of a person to the thought of his body; and, then, you are well on your slide to thinking of a person as a physical object; and, when that occurs, the thought of substance purrs into operation. This bracketing occurs in such mundane situations as counting the number of persons in your confirmation class or your Swingers Club. If someone asks you how many swingers are in the room, you very naturally count the number of human bodies there. You individuate the number of persons by individuating the number of bodies.

This bracketing habit may be broken by striking it on the anvil of other solid beliefs that you have. One of them is exploited in literary and dramatic works whose fulcrum is mistaken identity. In Shakespeare's *As You Like It*, for example, there are two pairs of persons whose identities are mistaken. Matters are very much mixed up in the play until the proper identities are re-established, after which the personae's emotions, actions, unexplained events, and plans fall neatly into place and a happy ending ensues. Authors who lever their works on the fulcrum of mistaken identity exploit the audience's belief that the identity of a person depends on his character, memories, affections, commitments, knowledge, past relations, habits and idiosyncrasies rather than on his body. It works this way. Suppose two persons whose identities are mistaken to have exactly similar bodies. If persons were just their bodies, we would think the play was much ado about nothing because there would be no point in agonizing, tragically or comically, about their identities since there is no difference between their bodies. But we, the audience, know there is much ado because there are important differences between them; they have different characters, memories, affec-

tions, and so forth. In sorting out identities, and faced with
similar bodies but different characters, memories, affections,
commitments, knowledge, past relations, habits, and idiosyncrasies—a set of features I call a persentity—the audience
chooses the latter as the mark of identity and, so, the core of
personhood; thus, instead of bracketing a person and his
body, you should bracket a person and his persentity. Since
as a member of Shakespeare's audience you already have this
habit, you should have no difficulty in dropping the contrary
habit of bracketing a person and his body. Once that habit is
dropped, you are sprung from the shackles of substance.

Reflection on a different situation, found frequently in science fiction stories, further confirms that you do have the
habit of bracketing a person and a persentity. Take the situation where there are two persons, this time with dissimilar
bodies as well as dissimilar persentities, who by some far out
means switch bodies and persentities. Where before Body A
and Persentity A' were associated, and Body B and Persentity
B' were associated, now Body A and Persentity B' are associated, and likewise for Body B and Persentity A'. Suppose a
woman were married to A-A', and suppose the author repre-
sents the woman as wishing to remain faithful to her husband,
and suppose the switch to have taken place. Which one should
the author have her choose as her husband, Body A-Persentity
B' or Body B-Persentity A'? The author will amuse you by
running through the confusing possibilities the switch entails
because he knows you know which one is really the husband.
Just think how amusing to read of the woman getting into bed
with Body A-Persentity B', thinking that she is getting into
bed with her husband (A-A'). And imagine how surprised
Body A-Persentity B' is at this unexpected, wayward bedfall.
Your amusement shows you do have the habit of bracketing
a person and a persentity. On the anvil of this habit, you can
break the contrary habit of bracketing a person and his body.

Another allied habit that reinforces your old metaphysical

habit is a grammatical one. If there is cutting, you believe there must be something that is cutting; if there is burning, there must be something that is burning; if there is falling, there must be something that is falling. Every predicate has a subject.

The something that is cutting may be a knife; the something that is burning may be a log; the something that is falling might be Galileo's balls. Knives, logs, and balls are physical objects; and lurking beneath them is physical substance. Oh grammar, oh substance, we feel thy sting!

That predicate-subject habit leads us to substance again when we consider some other verbs. Where there is wishing, there must be a wisher; where there is thinking, there must be a thinker; where there is smiling, there must be a smiler; where there is hoping, there must be a hoper. Are we not all subjects for our predicate verbs, we persons who wish, think, smile, and hope? And just as substance lurks beneath knives, logs, and balls, so we habituize, substance lurks beneath wishers, thinkers, smilers, hopers, beneath, in short, persons. We find ourselves, once again, in the grip of a grammatical habit that rubs our nose in substance.

Is there an anvil so strong that we may break this habit on it?

Yes, another strong grammatical habit. This habit forms around the verb "to have."

If a person is wishing, he *has* a wish; if he is thinking, he *has* a thought; if he is smiling, he *has* a smile; if he is hoping, he *has* hope. Thus far we might be tempted to think that what *has* a wish, a thought, a smile, or hope, is a person who is a substance, tempted, perhaps, to think he is a mental substance in the case of thinking, perhaps a combination of a mental and physical substance in the case of smiling (excepting Lewis Carroll's Cheshire cat who could grin even if the furry part disappeared). Further thought about our grammatical habit with "to have" can, however, help us resist the tempter.

We also say a person *has* a beautiful body, a good mind, a gentle soul. We can't say that someone has a beautiful body unless we are also willing to say he has a body; nor can we say he has a good mind unless we are willing to say he has a mind; nor can we say that he has a gentle soul unless we are willing to say he has a soul in some sense. We stroll a little farther down the grammatical path. If we say a person *has* a body, he can't *be* his body because a body doesn't "have" itself; and if we say a person *has* a mind, he can't *be* his mind because a mind doesn't "have" itself; and if we say a person *has* a soul, he can't *be* his soul because a soul doesn't "have" itself. The notion of a person can't be identified with body, mind, soul, or a combination of them because a person, according to our grammatical habit, "has" them but they can't "have" themselves.

Yet another form of temptation lurks behind this grammatical habit of attaching a person's predicates to a subject-substance, either physical or mental. We say "John is six feet tall" or "John is intelligent." This tempts us to infer from "is six feet tall" to "is his body" because we don't think we could say John is six feet tall unless John is his body. We wonder how John could have a bodily property if John is not his body. Similarly with "John is intelligent"; we are tempted to infer from "is intelligent" to "is his mind" because it doesn't seem possible for John to have a mental property unless he is his mind.

You can resist the wily tempter by holding the cross of "to have" before his face. Change "John is six feet tall" to "John's body is six feet tall"; after all, it is a body you are measuring. And when you measure John's intelligence, you are measuring something other than John because we say "John has an intelligent mind."

If a person isn't a body, or a mind, or a soul, or a combination of them, then we don't have to rub our nose in the physical or mental substance claimed to underlie them. The habit of moving, for example, from thinking to thinker to substance is broken on the anvil of the habit of moving from thinking to has a thought to has a mind to is not a mind (and so, to is not a mental substance).

In summary, the metaphysical habit of thinking of persons as substance can be broken on the anvils of two other habits, one, bracketing a person and a persentity and, two, the grammatical habit of "to have."

We know, though, that you may drift back to your old habit unless you have a satisfactory replacement. Let us move on now to the joyful task of making a different, morally and theoretically more useful vision of "the person."

Andrea suggested to Homer that a person may be more like a market than like a physical object. We know that Andrea had had too much brandy when she said that. Of course, it may be a ridiculous idea, but just on the chance that she was putting us on the trail of a vein we might profitably prospect, let's think about the notion of a market for a bit.

Here we are on a flying carpet, scooting over the world, peering down through its rents. We dip down toward the world to have a closer look. Below we see some things: two men, some pieces of silver, and a ham. The men are talking: "I'll give you five pieces of silver for the ham." "It's a deal. It's cheap, but a deal." We are witnessing an exchange which is a portion of a market.

An exchange is a banal occurrence that holds something of interest to us. The occurrence takes place amongst correlatives. A correlative is something—for example, a buyer—that stands in some relation to something else—for example, a seller—that stands in a relation to the buyer. Something that is a buyer is a correlative; it is a correlative to a seller. A parent and child are correlatives. A valley and a mountain are correlatives. Correlatives are tied with bonds of necessity. There cannot be a buyer unless there is a seller; and *vice versa*. There cannot be a parent unless there is a child; and *vice versa*.

There cannot be a valley without a mountain; and *vice versa.*

Just as a seller and a buyer are correlatives, so a seller and his goods are correlatives. One cannot be a seller unless he has goods to sell. Similarly, a buyer and his coin are correlatives. Also, a seller and the buyer's coin are correlatives because if the seller doesn't get something for his goods he has either given his goods as a gift or his goods have been stolen. Further, a buyer and the seller's goods are correlatives; you can't be a buyer if you haven't bought something.

The banal occurrence we call an exchange does not take place unless there are at least four things in a complex network of co-relations. A market such as the stock market is a set of such exchanges actual or potential.

One more step and then we will be ready to grasp a new vision of persons.

What makes silver (or seashells) money? Not the fact that it is silver, for something may be silver and not be money. Nor that it is valuable, for many things are valuable that are not money. What makes ham (or shoes) goods? It isn't always goods because sometimes it is food. What makes a person a buyer? Not that he is a person, for persons are not always buyers; sometimes they are sellers. Clearly, what makes silver money, ham goods, and persons buyers and sellers are their being in correlative relations to each other. It is not the silver's physical nature nor the ham's physical nature that makes one money and the other goods; their natures may make them silver and ham, but it is their co-relations that make them money and goods. (Hint: The concept of person is like the concepts of goods and money, not like the concept of ham or silver.)

In the spirit that we ask what makes an object such as ham a piece of goods, or what makes an object such as silver money, we ask what makes a body a person. We approach our answer to this question through an analogy. What makes a piece of wood a spear and a support and a part of a picture frame and a handle? The same piece of wood may be a spear to a boy playing Hercules, a part of a picture frame to an artist, a support for plants to the gardener, or a placard handle to a picketer.

Which of them the piece of wood is depends upon the situation it is in; it depends upon the relations it has to other things. Buyers, sellers, money, goods, spears, supports, picture frame parts, and handles are not things-in-themselves. They are what they are because of the other things to which they are related and because of the way they are related to those other things.

We can make this clearer by means of a generalization: xRy. We will let x and y stand for objects and R stand for a relation. Suppose y is a sheet of cardboard, x is the stick, and the relation R is "tacked to," so that the stick is tacked to the cardboard. That relation and the cardboard object to which the stick is related make the stick into a handle.

Suppose, again, that y is a willowy plant and the relation R is "tied to," so that the stick is tied to the plant. That relation and the plant to which the stick is related make the stick into a support.

x is a relatent, so I call it. What it is (a handle, a support, etc.) varies with and depends on R and y in xRy. y, too, I call a relatent.

Spears, supports, handles, picture frame parts, buyers, sellers, money, goods are relational entities, or what, in short, I call relatents. Let us call "xRy," as a whole, a relationship. x and y, considered together, I call correlatents; why I do so should be clear from my discussion of correlatives. In applying these notions to persons, I will call x the inner correlatent and y the outer correlatent.

Suppose that a piece of wood could simultaneously be a spear, a support, a picture frame part, a handle. It would be possible to give a name to the collection of these things; we could call the collection, for example, a ridotto. A person is like a ridotto. "Person" is the word we use to refer to a collection of relatents. Consider some of our relatents. There are familial relations that make us into sons, daughters, wives, fathers, uncles, and cousins. There are occupational relations that make us into bosses, employees, foremen, actors, salesman, assistant professors, longshoremen, journalists, executives, and lawyers. There are neighborhood relations that make us into neighbors, volunteers, Neighborhood Council members, Civic Affairs chairmen, monthly newsletter editors and writers, and boosters. There are city relations that make us taxpayers, voters, supervisors, citizens, mayors, witnesses, judges, Democrats, Republicans, jury members, and petitioners. A relatent is not the same concept as a role. I shall distinguish later between a factual– and a moral–relatent, which get confused in the concept of role.

Just as a piece of wood becomes a handle because relatents are created, that is, because it becomes related to other things in specific ways, so out of human bodies persons are created because their bodies become related to other bodies, families, occupations, neighborhoods, cities, and so forth. To be a person is to be many of the kinds of relatents of which I gave a sample list above. "Person" is the word we use to designate a collection of relatents. You are a collection of such relatents as son, husband, uncle, employee, musician, citizen, Democrat, voter, and many, many others.

This notion of person is theoretically useful because it helps us to understand what it means to say that man is a social being. Each person is a self; the self is a correlative being, a set of inner correlatents. Since a self is a collection of correlatents, and, since correlatents' existence and nature logically depend upon the existence of others and the nature of their relations to others, we see why the existence and nature of the self is logically dependent upon other persons; since other persons, too, are sets of correlatents, they, too, logically depend upon relations to your self and other selves.

You must not confuse this point with a commonplace psychological doctrine. It is a truism to say that our social environment influences the kind of attitudes, dreams, emotions, fears, ambitions, and conscience we have. My point is not a psychological one; it is a logical point. I am talking about the conditions necessary for your existence; and I am talking about the conditions necessary for your having the nature of a person at all, not about the psychological conditions that make you this kind of person rather than that kind of person.

This notion of person is theoretically useful, again, because it helps us to reinterpret our notion of society. We no longer have to think of a society as a collection of atoms, as a collection of hermetically sealed substances. A society is to self and others as a topography is to a mountain and a valley. A topography is a variation in land levels described relationally as mountains, valleys, and plains; a society is an organization of human bodies described relationally as sets of relatents. It is an arrangement that creates persons; some arrangements are good, others bad, because some make good persons possible and others do not.

The following two reality diagrams show us the contrast between a substance picture of social reality and a relatent picture of social reality.

Substance Picture of Society   Relatent Picture of Society

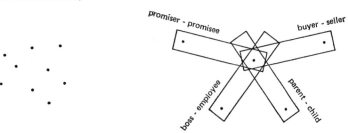

In the left diagram, a person is identified as a substance, represented by a dot. It is a picture of a reality composed of isolated substances. On the right, a person is identified as a

set of inner correlatents—promisee, employee, parent, and buyer. The outer correlatents in the picture are promiser, boss, child, and parent. It is a picture of a reality composed of persons. To picture a person in that diagram, we necessarily have to draw moral and social co-relations between the dots, which represent bodies. We can leave relations out of the substance picture of reality, however, because they are mere appearances in that world, whereas in the relatent world they are the reality of persons.

The substance picture underwrites the rugged individualist, who aims at self-sufficiency and maximum autonomy in pursuit of his self-interest. That picture posits the substance-dot as the moral center; all moral treasures are located there in the fortress self; and therein resides the autonomous, self-activating moral tyrant we call the will. The substance-dot defines the perspective from which he views the world; it affords him a personal point of view of the social landscape. From the safe battlements of the self, the tyrant directs his foraging forces of appearance in their raids on other appearances. Though his point of view is provincial, and though he is doomed to moral solipsism, he is happy enough because his vantage point is metaphysically autonomous, secure, and impregnable.

When we conceive of a person as a collection of relatents, it is impossible to locate the moral center in a dot. Since each inner correlatent requires an outer correlative entity, a person and his moral treasures are spread throughout the social landscape. A person cannot remain provincial in his point of view; he must take up the perspective of the other as well as himself because his existence and nature are logically related to the existence and nature of others. If, for example, you wish to be a seller, you must also concern yourself with the existence of a buyer; you must help some other to retain his buyer nature if you are to retain your seller nature. It is logically impossible to define a person's interests in terms of self-interest alone according to a relatent theory of persons; it is logically impossible to conceive of your interests apart from the interests of others; thus, the relatent theory is morally useful because it razes the rugged fortress walls of the substance-self.

The relatent notion of a person is morally useful also because it erases the distinction between a person's reality and his appearance, a distinction which is central to the substance notion of a person. In ranking the value of reality and appearance, reality takes chief place; appearance is "mere" appearance, illusion, the world's seeming, not its being. According to the substance theory, our character, including the social and moral aspects of our character, belong to appearance; our obligations to others and theirs to us are of secondary importance. This relegation of the social and moral aspects of our life to secondary importance gives free license to the rugged individualist who seizes the opportunity to pursue his "self-interest" with maximum autonomy. Restraint on one's action by others is to be avoided; obligations are a burden, not an opportunity—an obstacle, not a necessity.

With the relatent notion of a person, on the other hand, we can discern that our moral and social relations are both a necessity and an opportunity first, because they are necessary to our existence as persons, and secondly, because they are the material out of which we form our nature in accord with our ideal.

Perhaps another image might help you to grasp the concept of a person that I am advocating. Picture a net. Let the net represent a society, the net knots—not the string of the knots—represent persons, and the string between the net knots represent relations. If we were to cut the strings that lead from a net knot to other net knots, what was a net knot would become a detached, knotted string, but it would no longer be a net knot. (Moral: If you cut all a body's relations to other bodies, you have made relatents impossible for it and, thereby, destroyed a person [and injured the society]. Alienation is a form of murder.) What made the knotted string a net knot was its stringy relations to other net knots.

If I pull on a net knot some distance from a given net knot, the latter will be affected. (Moral: What is done to others in your society, whether done by you or someone else, is done to you.) Also, if someone pulls on a given net knot, it will affect the other net knots. (Moral: What is done to or by you is done to others in your society.)

And I will make you fishers of men.

8 MARBLEMAN AND THE NESTING RELATION

I prythee, Sire, playe no myggs wythe mye Sol.

—FANEBIUS PERLYNG

A person, being a collection of relatents, is unified when his relatents are unified. A unified person is created by a unified society. The complexity of a unified city is outlined by a skeletal structure that I call the nesting relation. I use the novel as an analogy to help us analyze the properties of the nesting relation.

❦ ❦ ❦

IF WE WERE TO explore fully the relatent theory of persons, we would have to explore how all such metaphysical ideas as Andrea and Homer discussed—beginning and end, individual, character, unity, change, identity, and interaction —apply to persons when a person is considered as a collection of relatents. In the last chapter, we touched on the notion of identity somewhat when we considered the idea of a persentity as a means of identifying persons; we saw that literature whose fulcrum is mixed identities relies on our habit of bracketing a person and a persentity.

In this chapter, we will consider a person's unity, and I will argue that it depends upon social unity.

When the question, "How may the Many be Many and also be One?" is asked about persons, it becomes, "How may the Many relatents be Many and also be One? How may the Many relatents of a person be unified so that the Many relatents make One person?" This is an important question for you because probably you are a sundered person. Not everyone is a whole, unified person. In fact, most of us are sundered in some respect or other. We don't quite completely hang together.

Here's the hard part for sundered sentimentalists to confront honestly: Becoming a whole, unified person, whatever theory of unity is offered, is not in your hands solely. The job of making a collection of relatents into a unified person depends in part upon others and the society in which you live. A fragmented society will thwart an individual's efforts to unify himself. Fragmented societies and sundered persons go together; unified societies and unified persons team it, too.

Now it's out as plain as a toad on new dinnerware. My obsession about a unified society is fed by the fear of our becoming Marblemen. I'm afraid you and I will end up a mere bag of marbles, that each of the relatents in our person-bag will be as glassily external and unconnected to each other as marbles. Should that be the case, we will never be unified, whole persons.

Refresh your image of the Relatent Picture of Social Reality printed in the previous chapter (page 76). Let me remind you of the terminology I introduced. "xRy" I called a relationship; "R" I called a relation; "x" and "y" I called relatents; together, "x" and "y" are correlatents; from the perspective of "x" as the self I called "x" the inner correlatent and "y" the outer correlatent; a person, I said, was a collection of inner correlatents. If we let "x" and "y" be the ends of a spoke, a person is the inner end or pole of the spoke and the thing to which he is related the outer end or pole of the spoke.

Since the correlatents, x and y, are logically tied together into a unity which we may call a correlatent unity, the relatents in a correlatent unity cannot be separated from each other without destroying the relatents. We can consider the outer correlatents to which a person's inner correlatents are tied as a Many and ask whether they are unified or sundered in relation to each other. If sundered, since an inner and an outer correlatent cannot be separated, the sunder wound between the outer correlatents is reflected in the inner correlatents; thus, the inner ones, too, will be sundered. When this fate befalls you, you become a schizophrenic person, a Marbleman. Because these outer correlatents together constitute component relatents of society, a sundered society slices its person members into sundered persons. There is nothing you can do to heal the slice in yourself unless you heal the slice in society. You cannot sew your sliced self together with your own bootlaces.

Here are some examples. Three inner correlatents are "head of a family," "leader of a neighborhood," and "mayor of a city." These inner correlatents cannot exist unless the three outer correlatents—a family, a neighborhood, and a city—also exist; each of these outer correlatents is, of course, a complicated entity made up of relatents in complex relations to each other. Unless the three outer relatents are unified, unless they compose a unified society, unless, in summary language, the family, its neighborhood, and the city are unified into a One, the inner correlatents will not be unified. Marblemen again.

Earlier, in Chapter 2, I gave a list of plagues associated with alienation, which showed that being an alienated person is not an attractive prospect. Being a Marbleman is no more attractive because he is a short step away from being an alienated man. Two considerations—identifying some progenitors of Marblemen and an escapist response to them—show us how easily we can back into our modern fate of alienation.

First, consider two progenitors of Marblemen, ethnocentrism and social contradiction. Ethnocentrism singles out some kinds of persons on an ethically irrelevant basis, isolates them, crams them into groups, gives them an "alien" character and less value than they give to the groups to which they themselves belong. When you want to unify your inner correlatents, you are faced with a disunified set of ethnocentrized outer correlatents that prejudiced persons prevent from being unified, thereby preventing you from unifying your matching inner correlatents. Examples of ethnocentrist prejudice are racism, nationalism, sexism, éliteism, snobbism, patriotism, and classism.

Another fertile progenitor of Marblemen is a society's inner contradictions. As a student relatent a person may have been taught all about "democratic equality and tolerance" while as a Black occupational relatent he has a hard time finding a job. As a citizen relatent you are fed big with the importance of thinking for yourself and speaking your mind but as an offspring relatent you may find your mother or father urging you toward conformity so you can "get ahead." Outer correlatents may make contradictory demands on you.

It would be utopian to anticipate an Armageddon in which ethnocentrism and contradictions would be vanquished totally and finally. We know that the struggle against the Marbleman tide is unending. There can be no hope of a final victory. In the face of such a prospect, it is easy to lose courage and the will to fight; it is easy to try an escape route.

An obvious, tempting, frequently evoked escape response to these two progenitors of Marblemen is withdrawal. Instead of continuing to try to unify the outer correlatents that have been divided by ethnocentrism and contradiction, many simply withdraw from them, abandon them to the prejudiced and to contradiction. This escapist response has another name —alienation, or more accurately, self-alienation since it is self-imposed alienation. For example, a disunity in your person between the inner correlatents created by your family relations and the inner correlatents created by your city relations can be escaped by cutting off your city relations, by alienating yourself from your city. The effect of this self-alienation is to destroy those of your inner correlatents whose existence depends upon your being related to the city.

It is obvious, then, that alienating yourself, cutting off relations with social entities and other persons, is a self-destructive solution to disunity. It cuts you down, diminishes you, blocks your way toward full self-realization and the good life.

We are now in a position to understand why alienation has the associated plagues I listed, and to compute the emotional price of being an escapist Marbleman.

We feel socially ineffective, excessively self-centered, and suffer truncated benevolence because self-alienation is giving up the fight; it is a turning away from outer tasks; we try to mask our shame with the bravado of rugged individualism, whose consequences, we saw, are morally disastrous.

We feel socially aimless, morally confused, and inhibit our commitment because we do not face and dialectically resolve the social contradictions amidst which we live.

We agonize through the insecurity of not having shared, socially confirmed convictions and we drown in ungrounded suspicions and fears because all about us we observe the same self-alienation escapism in our fellow citizens. Mutual withdrawal is not complementary but mutually defeating.

In case self-destructive paring down and its remorseless pathology isn't your cup of existence, in case you want to reach full self-realization, you have no other alternative but courageously to concinnate, to help create a bigotless, non-contradictory society. Self-imposed alienation is the coward's escape from the social butchers that slice, chop, and saw your personhood into disconnected bits.

Any philosopher who tells you that you can't be unified and whole until we create a unified society has the responsibility of trying to describe the outlines, at least, of what we should try to create, especially after doing in as many unity theories as I did in Chapter 5. I turn to that description now.

The society I advocate, of course, has for its polity the city-state. To depict its general structure, I shall use the novel as our model, which is appropriate, because in the creation of a city that will create good persons, we should expect analogical mileage by selecting a creative work's structure as our analogical guide. Besides, a novel is a creative work whose structure is relatively well known to us, and it has a richness of parts and a useful complexity.

The overall structure of a novel exhibits what I shall call the nesting relation; it is a complex relation that consists of four other relations—serial, disonion, differential, and mutuality relations.

The *serial* relation is illustrated by the serial order of the components: letter-word-sentence-paragraph-chapter-novel. It is this relation that enables us to say that a novel contains ten chapters, or that chapter six has a lot of offensive sentences in it; it also prevents us from saying that the sentence literally contains too many paragraphs.

It should be obvious that this analogous serial order of components obtains: person-family-neighborhood-city.

We must resist the temptation to think of the serial order of novels' and cities' components as if they were stages in a series of more and more inclusive containments, as if a city contained a neighborhood, a neighborhood contained families, and families contained persons. By this reasoning, a city would contain a person and we would then be led to think that a person is part of a city. Such an inclusive containment series would over-simplify the nesting relation; it suits an onion, where each successive layer contains the immediately preceding layer and all other preceding layers, but it doesn't suit a novel, nor an interesting city. Each layer of onion is still onion, but each successive component of a novel and city is unlike the preceding components. A word is unlike a sentence, which is unlike a paragraph, and so forth. This unlikeness of components in the series I call the *disonion* relation.

There is a close connection between the disonion property of the nesting relation and its *differential* property. Our examination of the disonion property showed us that the various components in the nesting relation series are unlike one another; hence, the various components will call for different unifying relations. We can illustrate this with the components of a novel's series. The relation that unifies letters into words is different from the relation that unifies words into sentences; we speak of spelling words but not of spelling sentences; we speak of ungrammatical sentences but not of ungrammatical paragraphs. In order to construct a novel, we need a relation unifying letters into words, a different one unifying words into sentences, still a different one unifying sentences into paragraphs, another for unifying paragraphs into chapters, and still another for unifying chapters into a novel. The relation holding among this series of differing unifying relations I call the differential relation.

Applying the differential relation to cities, we recognize that the relation between component persons that unifies them into a family is different from the relation that unifies component families into a neighborhood, both of which are different from the relation that unifies component neighborhoods into a city. Parenthetically, in this essay I address myself only to the relation unifying neighborhoods into a city, which, as I said earlier, is the relation of social understanding.

The disonion and differential properties can teach us something about the part-whole relation. Much discussion of social unity is unproductive, over-simplified, and downright confusing because it is dominated by the part-whole vocabulary. The part-whole vocabulary leads thinkers to suggest the wrong structure for social units, to over-simplify actual relations that presently obtain, and to avoid an analysis that clarifies the task of constructing a rich social unity.

If the disonion and differential complexity of the nesting relation were ignored, it would seem to make obvious sense for someone to ask for the principle that explains how words are unified into a novel. Of course, there is no such principle. The unifying relation between words will reveal how words combine into sentences, but not how they will combine into a novel; we learn that from the disonion and differential properties. The part-whole vocabulary, however, appears to make the request for the principle that unifies words into novels perfectly sensible because that vocabulary allows us to say that words are parts of novels. There is nothing in the part-whole notion *per se* that prevents it. My proposal here leads us to revise and sophisticate the part-whole language. We can say that words are parts of a sentence, but we cannot say that words are parts of a novel, nor of a paragraph, nor of a chapter. Chapters, indeed, are parts of a novel because they are components of a stage immediately preceding the novel stage.

More generally, each stage save the first in the letter-word-sentence-paragraph-chapter-novel series is a One that has Many parts drawn from the immediately preceding stage only; they are not parts of any other stage.

Although we cannot say that words are parts of a novel, nor that sentences are, nor that paragraphs are, we can say that they nest in novels. Words, for example, can nest in the novel because they are parts of sentences which are parts of paragraphs which are parts of chapters which are parts of novels.

By analogy, we learn to discern that a city's parts are its neighborhoods. Neither persons nor families are parts of the city. Persons are parts of families; families are parts of neighborhoods. Persons nest in neighborhoods and cities. This can be said because of the disonion and differential properties. In the past, theorists of social unity have tried to schedule society's unity by providing unifying relations between persons, thinking that persons are parts of society. The contract theory shows this error rather clearly. Howsoever many components we wish to introduce into the nesting relation series, I suggest that the disonion and differential properties warn us that the structure of society is far more complex than the simple part-whole relation would lead one to believe.

In addition to its serial, disonion, and differential properties, the nesting relation has a *mutuality* property. To the novel reader it is obvious that the replacement of some sentences with others would have an influence on the novel, particularly if the replacement occurs in key places. To the novel writer it is obvious that the direction of influence runs not only from the smaller to the larger stages in the letter-word-sentence-paragraph-chapter-novel series but also in the other direction, from the larger to the smaller stages. The smaller and the larger stages have mutual influence.

The writer's conceptions of the novel as a whole, and of its chapters, and of the chapters' paragraphs, guide him in the construction of his sentences. There are, after all, an infinite number of sentences which the writer could have written. He must have some principles of sentence selection if the book is not to be a random collection of sentences.

Consider the most important sentence in Henry Fielding's novel, *Tom Jones*. It comes after the good Mr. Allworthy has discovered that his trusted nephew Blifil has been villainously deceiving him about Tom. Blifil's deception is so shocking and offensive to Mr. Allworthy that the good man bids "the servant tell Blifil that he [Allworthy] knew him not." And now comes the most important sentence in the novel: " 'Consider, dear sir,' cries Jones, in a trembling voice." (Book XVII, Chapter XI)

Few sentences could more tellingly show Tom's unbounded power of forgiveness, nor more convincingly prove Tom's goodness. Fielding's conception of his novel, of his mode of representing a prodigiously generous, forgiving person, of the means of expressing his own views about forgiveness, guided him in writing that sentence.

The property of mutuality can be shown by another example. Suppose Tom Jones' sentence in another context. Suppose a widower who has just suffered grievous financial losses to be standing in a miserable bedroom housing all his children, each racked with a fatal, mysterious illness, saying with a hopeless wave of his arms to his creditor who has just asked for the repayment of a loan, "Consider, dear sir." Here the identical sentence has quite another effect.

In the same way that the writer's conception of the whole novel influences his construction of the sentences, paragraphs, and chapters that nest in his novel, so the conception of the ideal city will influence the creator of the city in his choice and design of the components which, when unified, will constitute the ideal city he desires.

So, you see, dear Mishkin, I haven't forgotten you. All the while I was discussing the nesting relation, you thought I had put you out of my mind. Nothing could be further from the truth. I have never thought of you more intensely than when I thought of the nesting relation, for I was preparing the womb of your rebirth. In considering the social units which help create the inner correlatents of which you are made, and in considering the nesting relation, I was laying hands on the very structure in which the new you will come into existence, Mishkin. Think of a person and his inner correlatents as a microcosm of the outer correlatents that, when unified, will constitute your city. In drawing blueprints of your city, we were also drawing blueprints of you.

You who hunger for a sense of community hunger to nestle in a city structured by the nesting relation. You hunger for that feeling which steals over you when you feel at One, when your inner and outer correlatents are nesting concinnately together, when that old devil Marbleman is laid away and you are reborn as One.

In summary, in this chapter I have sketched the Marbleman syndrome, given examples of his progenitors, showed how self-destructive self-alienation is, urged you to fight the Marbleman drift in the only way possible, namely, by creating a unified society; I claimed that was the only way because logically your inner correlatents' unity is dependent upon the outer correlatents' unity; courage, Mishkin; and to give you an indication of the complexity of the task, I outlined the nesting relation, which showed, among other things, that a society is unified by different relations at different levels; the search for a single principle of civil unity is a gross, mistaken, oversimplification.

The main point of this chapter is my siren call to action. In order to become the person you want to be, you must change the world. That *you* must change the world should be obvious to you if you resent control over your person. The nature of your inner correlatents depends in part on the nature of the outer correlatents. What is the consequence, Mishkin, if someone else controls and shapes your outer correlatents? That's right; he controls and shapes you. Do not be fooled by consciousness-oil salesmen: Altering your consciousness will not alter the nature of your outer correlatents!

Everything depends on being your own artificer, then. The paradox of that is the subject of the next chapter.

9 YOU, AS TRANSCENDENTAL ARTIFICER

Flye uppe, deare Byrd, and roost yn Hevyn.
—FANEBIUS PERLYNG

My thesis in this chapter is that persons may be transcendent rather than immanent, that they may by their own hand escape the cage of nature, create and remake themselves, and become an ornament to the world.

🏵 🏵 🏵

I HAVE ARGUED that a person is a collection of relatents. Babies are animal bodies that become persons when they become related to such social units as other persons, families, neighborhoods, and cities.

The inner correlatents that constitute the building blocks of your person will vary depending on the kind of relations you have to those social units and on the nature of those social units (xRy). This means that the nature of your city is personally important to you because the nature of the city to which you relate will determine the nature of your own person. Although you have to make yourself indirectly by first remaking your outer correlatents, that is, by remaking your society, still, I am advocating that you be your own artificer and your own product, and not forget the "self" in "self-realization." This call to make ourselves may seem to be an obvious course as well as a suitably stirring one, but we should not let our self-congratulation lull us into a thoughtless acquiescence to the intellectual "obviousness" of this recommended course. The "obviousness" may rest on quicksand provided by commonsense, be contradicted by reigning scientific theory, or be challenged by logical impossibility.

First, I want to call attention to three bogs of commonsense quicksand: free will, misemphasis on the uniqueness of personality, and a cliché conception of human institutions.

The idea that each man is in charge of his own destiny, suffering or enjoying the consequences of his karma, is familiar to us from the doctrine of free will. For those who believe we have free will, it seems obvious that we must make ourselves, that we alone are responsible for what we will become. However, this is romantic exaggeration of the will's ability to create the inner correlatents of which persons are made. I repeat, our inner correlatents are logically tied to outer correlatents and the existence and nature of each inner correlatent depends on the nature of its outer correlatent and the kind of relation holding between them. These outer correlatents may be very complex, as a city is, for example; obviously, the nature of a city is as dependent upon other persons' aims and relations as it is on yours. You cannot solely by an act of your own will change the nature of the complex outer correlatents; they are changed by acts of cooperation, whether freely or forcibly enacted. Think of a wondrous, plastic material; let that be you. Think now of a mother mold; let that be the social units, the outer correlatents, to which you are related. The plastic material is shaped by the mold. In order to produce a differently shaped you deliberately, you *and others* must change the mold consciously and cooperatively. Thus, we have to think past our own power of free will in order to comprehend what being our own artifact entails; "obviously," the obviousness of making ourselves cannot rest solely on our being blessed (or damned) with a free will, even supposing we had such a will.

A second bog of commonsense quicksand is the pride we take in having or developing a unique personality and/or character. This has been lifted out of the commonsense realm and dignified by philosophical existentialists, who hold that man's existence precedes his essence. According to them, man, unlike other entities, does not come into existence with a fixed species nature; there is no such thing as human nature that defines man as man. By our own acts we give ourselves a nature; we make our own essence. According to Jean-Paul Sartre, "If man, as the existentialist conceives him, is indefinable, it is because at first he is nothing. Only afterward will he be something, and he himself will have made what he will be. . . . Man is nothing else but what he makes of himself. Such is the first principle of existentialism. It is also what is called subjectivity. . ."

The pervasive wish to choose and form our own personality-character, and the near universal desire that it be unique and not be stamped out by the common die of "human nature" has made a popular form of existentialism a fashionable philosophy. This philosophy has articulated a basis for human dignity by distinguishing human subjectivity from and elevating it above the objective facticity of inert objects and lower animals. I note, simply, that this is a quicksand basis for thinking that "obviously" we should and must make ourselves; our thinking must seek solider ground than this; in my discussion of the concept of person, I have not been talking about personality and character formation and their uniqueness; I have been talking about person *per se*. Before there can be personality, unique or otherwise, there must be person. Unlike a popular form of existentialism, I do not think we can assume the existence of person and concentrate on his essence formation. The prior metaphysical task is to understand the conditions necessary for the existence of man as person. To account for the existence of person, we have to go beneath human subjectivity into human collectivity, because our inner correlatents are logically tied by bonds of necessity to the outer correlatents of human collectivity.

The third bog of quicksand in which the "obviousness" of having to make ourselves sinks out of sight is a cliché conception of social institutions. People often assume that social institutions are products of man's design and effort. This notion, combined with my emphasis on the role of outer correlatents in creating persons, would seem to make it "obvious that we "should" create ourselves because, already being in control of our social institutions, we now are doing just that. In fact, however, social institutions and changes are seldom consciously planned, constructed, or controlled by man. Institutions generally change or mutate or disappear without the stir of a single forethought. Consider the withering away of the extended family. An extended family consists of at least three generations of persons in functioning relations; and it may consist of cousins, uncles, second cousins, great-aunts, etc. The extended family members may or may not live in the same domicile; if not housed together, they may function as a family by sending each other money, operating a business together, or housing a brother's son while he attends college. Extended families have been disappearing in American cities. In small, rural communities where the members' interests are nearly similar—the weather, livestock, farm crops, last Sunday's sermon—because their occupations are nearly similar, some extended families still survive. But in our Great American Cities there is too great a variety in jobs to sustain similar life-long interests, and the training and education for those jobs aren't tied to an apprenticeship with Dad, doing as Dad does. The variety of interests which city folk develop leads them to seek their intimate and functioning relations with people who aren't relatives. Thus does the extended family dwindle to the immediate nuclear family, itself, in turn, hard pressed.

This change in our social fabric was not planned nor consciously executed as we plan or make an artifact; the extended family was not evaluated and found wanting or desirable, whichever might be the case, and social control exercised in accord with that evaluation. To the extent to which a similar account could be given of the development, demise, and change of other social institutions, to that extent our society is not a deliberately produced artifact, and, so, to that extent, another commonsense ground for the "obviousness" of making ourselves sinks with barely a trace.

In summary, my call to create ourselves should not be conceived as obvious if that is based on the three common-sense grounds that I have just discussed. None of those grounds are any firmer basis than quicksand for presenting you with a justified demand that you make yourself.

Secondly, turning to the reigning scientific theory, we find that it not only renders it unobvious that we should make ourselves, we find that it denies we can. Consider the distinction between the "natural" and the "artificial." Most English speakers know they are exclusive terms; they know that what is artificial is not natural and that what is natural is not artificial. They also know that "artificial," in one of its senses, means "that which man makes by his art." Artifacts are things consciously made by man. An artificial bridge is an artifact. A natural bridge on the other hand is one that has come into being by the action of wind, water, ice, geologic upheaval, or some other natural, that is, non-human force.

The most cursory review of the intellectual trend in the West reveals a drift toward the naturalization of man and away from ideas that would support the view that he is a product of either God's or his own artifice. Consider.

✻　✻　✻

Once upon a time, men believed that there was a God who created the world. This God was a Great Artist. He fashioned and brought the world into being even as you and I fashion and make our trousers or an aeolian harp. His greatest triumph was man whom He made in His own image.

What is it, many asked, to be made in His image? In answer it was said, "To be transcendent as He is, to be outside of nature." "It is easy," they replied, "to think of God as transcendent, for he was before the world and outside it just as we are before and outside the harp which we make. But we neither were before nor did we make the world."

In answer it was said, "To be transcendent as He is is to have a soul. Nothing created, other than man, has a soul; having an immortal soul enables man to exist outside nature when his natural body goes the way of all flesh." But then there came biologists and anthropologists who saw man's evolution from and continuity with other animals which everyone knew were part of nature, and "So," they said, "man too must be part of nature."

In answer it was said, "There is nature and non-nature, and man is not in nature because he is transcendent. To be transcendent as He is is to have free will. Free will enables us to act free of the domination of natural forces and natural laws. Apes do not have free will; that is why they are part of nature." But then there came psychologists and sociologists who replied, "When we study man we use the same scientific method that other scientists use in their study of volcanoes, atoms, bees, chimpanzees, and Russian dogs. We can use the same method because we are interested in the natural forces which govern man just as geologists are interested in the natural forces which govern volcanoes. Man can no more escape nature and nature's laws than can rocks and acid."

And then in that time some became more aggressive against transcendence. They were not content merely to take man out of non-nature and to put man into nature. They wanted to empty transcendental non–nature of all its content. "Let us," they said, "decapitalize god." And the some became many, and they said, "We do not need the great artist for we do not need a non-natural creation story." With one-half of the nature-non–nature distinction emptied, no one bothered to snuff the fire; the distinction burned, and only the "nature" half was left standing, and man was immanent.

✿　✿　✿

Well, is man natural? Is it possible for him to be artificial? My sketch of the intellectual trend indicates that he is natural and cannot be artificial because the attempt to make him transcendent to nature apparently fails. He appears to be within nature, and, being immanent, is subject to the same dominating laws as everything else that is immanent, which is everything else, and is as much a natural effect of natural forces as they.

It is possible to argue, and this is the third and strongest challenge to the "obviousness" of the call for self-creation, that it is logically impossible for man to make himself. This argument can be developed from an analysis of the concept of an artificer, within which lies embedded the concept of transcendence. Our sketch of the naturalization of man prepared us for this relation between the concepts of artificer and transcendence.

Consider the following analysis of the concept of artificer. I mention only what seem clearly logically necessary ingredients of the concept.

An artificer (a) works with material
                (b) to make a product;
                (c) the artificer and his product are not identical, as a cabinet maker and the cabinet are not identical;

(d) the artificer exists prior to the product
(e) and outside the product;
(f) the material is changed and/or rearranged
(g) by the exercise of intelligence and skills
(h) according to a plan
(i) with the aim of producing something of more value to someone than the material from which it is made.

The concept of transcendence I take to involve at least the elements (c), (d), and (e) of the analysis, which, you notice, are embedded in the concept of artificer. Now someone could argue that it is logically impossible for man to be his own artificer. His first premise would be to point out that, schematically, to say that a man makes himself is to say "M makes M." But for his second premise he could refer to the (c) part of our analysis and point out that according to it the maker and his product are not identical; however, we do find this identity assumed in the first premise (M makes M); therefore, the concept of artificer makes it contradictory to call for something to be its own product. Similar arguments can be extracted from the other "transcendence" elements, (d), and (e) because one can ask with respect to (d) how M can exist prior to itself; or with respect to (e) how M can be outside itself. These are all logical absurdities; they show that an artificer cannot transcend himself; therefore, not only is it unobvious that we should be our own products, it is logically impossible for us to be our own products—unless we can find a way to avoid this conclusion.

I believe that despite the scientific naturalization of man and the argument against the logical coherence of self-transcendence, we can justify advocating that man create himself because I believe we can answer both of these arguments.

With respect to the scientific naturalization of man, I shall argue that man is both transcendent and immanent. To the extent that he is transcendent, he can be an artificer. With respect to the argument that it is contradictory to suppose he can be his own artificer, I shall argue that by distinguishing between a present and future self we can avoid the contradiction.

I show first in what sense man transcends nature. For this, we need to distinguish two kinds of order; one is the order of natural events and the other is the order of thought, the latter being a part of the concept of an artificer, (g). The order of thought is embedded in language; when you learn a language, you are learning an orderly system of signs. Nature, too, has an order; you have learned to adapt to it; you sharpen your knife to cut a roast; you fill your tank with gasoline to make your car run; you open your umbrella to keep you dry on rainy days.

Consider the crossroads of these two orders: the human head. Consider light being reflected off an object and through an eye's pupil in that head; the optic nerve is excited and this, in turn, causes events to occur in the brain, thereby producing a visual image. So far we have events happening according to a natural order. Consider, now, relating those natural images to your language, that is, consider someone using his linguistic system to describe what he has seen. We have two things of moment to us here: the natural image and the sentences describing that image. The natural image falls within the natural order and is related to other natural events; but the sentence falls within the order of thought and is related to other sentences.

The sweep of language is wide. Even the order of nature is expressible in language; sentences can express the laws of nature. Once the order of nature is reflected in a language's sentences, that natural order has a counterpart in the order of thought because those sentences are subject to the order of thought. The order of thought is the order of logical relations between sentences. For example, one sentence implies another, and it contradicts still another. The laws of logic, which express the order of thought, are not natural laws; they do not order sentences causally as natural laws order natural events. Laws of logic are rules for valid, rational thought.

Since the laws of logic are different from the laws of natural events, they must express an artificial, not a natural, order. When man reflects rationally, when he thinks validly, that is, when he thinks in accord with the rules of logic, he is free of the tyranny of natural forces because he has adopted the order of artificial rules. When he does this, he has transcended nature; he has escaped the bonds of natural orders; he is no longer immanent, no longer a mere system of natural events.

Someone might point out that if there are only these two orders, we must think by the order of nature because we don't always think logically; that is, we don't always think in accord with the order of logic.

This is an important observation and forces us to the next point which is really the fulcrum of man's transcendence, namely, his ability to correct himself; using the fulcrum of self-correction, man can lever himself out of the kind of immanence in which all other kinds of entities are caged.

The ability to correct ourselves depends upon language. First, by being able to put our thoughts into language, we make our thought an object for further thought; and, secondly, by self-consciously expressing the order of thought in language as valid rules of logic, we make the rules an object of thought; we can, thirdly, compare our actual thought with the logical rules. Finally, should we find our actual thought out of accord with the rules, this additional bit of information can be fed back into our thought and, so, used to alter our original actual thought; this process can be repeated so the new, altered thought can be put in accord with logic; we will then have corrected ourselves and escaped the original natural order that produced the first, faulty thought.

We can compare the rules of logic with a ruler and our actual thought with an object to be measured. The ruler enables us to measure the object and determine how we are to alter it to make it the length we want just as we can use logical rules to determine how to alter our thought until it "measures up." I have emphasized the importance of putting our thought in language because this is what makes it and preserves it as an object for further thought and, so, a candidate for correction.

In summary, man's transcendence over the tyranny of natural law turns on his self-correcting abilities, which, in turn, are ours because through the use of language we can make our thought and its ruler objects for ourselves.

Even though we may have shown satisfactorily that man transcends nature in the sense that he can escape being blindly run by natural laws like entities without language are because he can correct himself, and, thus, purposively guide his activity as an artificer does, we still have to show that it is logically possible for him to be his own artificer.

We can show it is logically possible if we can escape from the identity of M in "M makes M." This identity led us into contradiction because the concept of transcendence would not permit the identity of artificer and product. We can escape the identity by making a distinction between the present person and the future person. If we think of the first M in "M makes M" as the present person (Mp) and the second M as the future person (Mf), we get "Mp makes Mf," or "The present self makes the future self." We no longer have an identity of artificer and product if we use this distinction and, hence, circumvent the contradiction; further, this captures the way we do change ourselves and fits in with the self-correction notion of transcendence that I just sketched.

Once again, this self-correction is possible because by linguistically describing a potential, better, future self we make a ruler against which to measure the present reality of ourselves; if we do not "measure up," our future-person ruler gives us the standard we need to alter ourselves appropriately.

We have gone through some heavy theoretical brush in this chapter, trying, first, to show that the obvious grounds for thinking we should be our own artificer and product are not as obvious as they seem because they—free will, uniqueness of personality, and illusion about our past and present control over social institutions—do not provide grounds for the metaphysical self-creation that I am recommending. Secondly, I have tried to show that man can transcend nature despite the reigning scientific trend that makes man immanent and despite the logical challenge to self-creation.

This theoretical abstract excursus has not been a useless, Byzantine exercise. Meeting the challenge of science and logic has shown us that practice must be informed by theory. We learned that man can be transcendent and be his own artificer only because he is self-correcting. Self-correction, however, requires the use of a standard, an ideal measure, either of logic or of a conceived future self; therefore, man cannot transcend nor deliberately improve himself unless he knows what he wants to be. That is the precise point of this essay, to move us closer toward a vision of our ideal, future self so that in measuring ourselves against what we would be, we can know how we must correct ourselves in order to attain that ideal. Once we have that ideal standard, it is possible to climb outside the cage of nature, and when the early spasm of pleasure in our transcendental freedom has subsided, we can settle down to a rewarding, informed, practicing autonomy.

We should learn that the stirring call to create a better self is practical only if we philosophically depict the good life, the ideal self, and the good society. This is the premier task in thinking about the city and takes high precedence over talk about zoning laws, speeded-up traffic, tax rates, police dogs, road widening, the inevitability of megalopolis, electing a new mayor, redevelopment, rapid transit, code enforcement, and such matters. Without theory, practice is blind; because our practice has been a stranger to theory, we have inherited civic chaos.

Thus far in this essay, the reader will have gotten the impression that I think that man has only an intellectual nature, as if I did not think he has an emotional life; this would be true except for my references to the plagues associated with alienation. In the next chapter, I address myself to the emotional side of our civic existence. I tie the concept of person that I have been developing into the emotional sense of community.

10 THE CITY AS A WORK OF ART

Stadtluft macht frei.
　　—JOHANNES F. PERLYNG

Transcendent persons authoring a city, using the nesting relation as a guideline, should aim to so flesh that skeleton that the created city will elicit in its inhabitants the emotional sense of community appropriate in a dynamic city. This affective result can be garnered by fashioning a city in which the inhabitants may become citizens, that is, one in which every inhabitant has equal and easy access to power.

❦　❦　❦

THAT OUR STATES OF feeling and our emotions are relevant to the good life does not seem to require argument. In the first part of this chapter, I indict our present institutions for doing nothing at best and at worst destroying any civil, civic emotions. In the second part, I identify the sense of community as a desired and desirable civic emotion, characterize such a sense that would be appropriate for a modern city, and explain how it can be aroused if we treat the city as a work of art.

Some intellectual products of our age are welcomed and fitted into the scheme of our society. At least those intellectual products that can be fitted into the technology of business and government are welcomed. Profit and (fire) power prosper with the aid of scientific technology. Grants, subsidies, subcontracts, prime contracts, research facilities, automation, and computerization, are part of the growing jargon of the knowledge-industrialists and politicians. They are the means for channeling knowledge and knowledge capital.

Are business and government coping this effectively with our emotional output? What are they doing to weave our emotions into a rewarding social pattern? The main thing they're doing is inflating our incipient greed and fear so we can be harnessed for profit and combat, and deflating our righteous anger so no one else can harness that power. It takes no keen-eyed critic of business to detect its heavy investment in human emotions. What do people do with their time when they aren't working? They read newspapers, magazines, look at billboards or listen to the radio while commuting, or watch television. Who pays the freight for these media? Businesses that advertise their products. Those advertisements have a single aim: to increase the sale of products. They increase sales by inflating acquisitive emotions into, preferably, greed. No temperance, please, just encourage a consumer variation on one of the seven deadly sins.

Neither does it take a highly perceptive observer of government to detect the extent of our national government's interest in citizens' emotions. Fear has gotten a big play; bureaucrats and politicians have inflated apprehension about political changes wrought and promised by socialism, communism, and hippies into a ravening, hot-eyed, loud-mouthed, intemperate, abject, mind-bending fear. Both political parties have seen the usefulness of harnessing fears of youth, revolutionaries, and communism to pull their little, blank, white, and blue political wagons.

The Democrats have been relative wizards, the Republicans reluctant adepts, at deflating the righteous anger of the poor, the unemployed, the minorities, the untrained, the old, the sick in mind and body, the victims of obsolescence, and all those others who have reason to inflate their anger into a revolutionary fervor.

The Democrats hit on the idea of using social services as a way of increasing their political power without threatening those who have no need of anger. They understand the psychology of Christmas basket charity and have simply organized it into the routine of taxes. Governmental social services provide the amelioration to gloss the continuous economic and social depression which the majority of Americans suffer.

There are two other organized bodies besides business and government and one disorganized body which attempt to structure our emotions. The two organized bodies are the schools and the church, and the disorganized body is composed of artists.

The churches fall outside the scope of this essay except to the extent that they have made themselves as much Caesar's instrument as Christ's. The church is mainly *status quo* on civic emotions. The exceptions are those scattered priests, ministers, rabbis and bishops who have tried to shake off the animus and torpor of church bureaucrats by supporting civil rights movements, peace makers, the poor, and hairy people.

The public schools presently organize, tame, and leach the emotions of children so they will grow to be tractable employees. Colleges and universities do the same for job trainees and the vestigial liberal art lovers who upon graduation will enter the business world, or teach, or work at jobs unrelated to their education. Except that colleges and universities put themselves at the service of government or industry, they play no other significant role in organizing civic emotions. The emergence of educational activists against racism, irrelevance, and authoritarianism in colleges and universities offers some hope if their energy becomes creative and if they are able to sustain themselves. Related to this is "continuing education" which, if properly developed beyond its present infantile stage, could come to something.

Historically, art (and when I use this word I do not mean sculpture and the graphic arts alone, but also film, drama, music, poetry, creative writing, opera, mime, dance, and the various crafts) has been a means of organizing thought and emotions. The chart of art's success reveals a wave-like line, its peaks occurring when artists have possessed the informal organization spun off by a strong civic purpose, the troughs occurring when they serve the narcissistic cant of romantic self-expression and/or when they jockey for position in the market place. When art is important to a society and address-es the civic emotions of the citizens, it is the most significant way of organizing a wide array of emotions; when art isn't important to society it only inflates the artist's private emo-tions or caters to the economic excesses of the monied. The persisting candlepower of the art produced during past Gold-en Ages promises that the arts of our own day may, if turned on, illuminate our own *civitas obscura*. I have more to say about art and its civic function in Chapter 14.

I said at the beginning of this chapter "that our states of feeling are relevant to the good life does not seem to require argument," but someone might argue that our sense of well-being, or its opposite, are not identical to fleeting, momentary emotional states. I reply that at least one feeling is not fleeting nor momentary, and is, I claim, a major ingredient of our sense of well-being. This is the sense of community; its importance as an ingredient of a sense of well-being is easily grasped be-cause it is the antithesis of the emotional pathology of aliena-tion and its associated plagues.

It is not difficult to explain why a sense of community is stable and durable enough to be the ingredient I claim it is. Emotions and feelings are responses to apprehended objects, acts, states of affairs, or events. The intellectual apprehension of any one of them will affect which emotion is aroused and how intensely it is felt. Seeing a soldier from a hiding place and apprehending him as an enemy will arouse fear while apprehending him as an ally will arouse relief; the degree to which he appears capable of harm or help will affect the intensity of these emotions. The duration of an emotion will depend on the duration of the object, act, state of affairs, or event arousing it, or on the duration of our apprehension of them; and its stability will depend on the stability of the apprehended entity arousing it or in the stability of our apprehension of it. These objective and subjective conditions of emotions explain why a sense of community may be of sufficient duration and stability to be a significant ingredient of the good life, because if we were to live in a unified, stable, just, tolerant, complex city, we would be continually apprehending and interacting with cooperative social correlatents and participating in civic events; this would help sustain a sense of well-being because continual support from such a city would continually and reliably arouse a sense of community.

Given that a sense of community is an emotional pay-off at which we should aim, it is important to indicate briefly how the unity of a city contributes to this sense of community. A society, being a complex entity, consists of a number of constituent entities; apprehension of a city will arouse a complex emotion because, in apprehending its constituent entities, we will respond with emotions and feelings to each of them. A city that is not unified will harbor constituents that produce social contradictions; these contradictory outer correlatents will arouse conflicting, contrary emotions. There may be a contradiction between, for example, your church's moral standards and your mayoral candidate's moral standards; consequently, your emotional response to them will be conflicted. Because the church and the candidate cannot both fit into a communal unity unless the contradiction between them is overcome, our emotional response to them cannot be a sense of community.

The sense of community is felt by fewer and fewer persons in our society. The American transition from a rural to an urban population, a transition still in progress, has created a sense-of-the-city crisis, because, while increasing the need for this sense, it has simultaneously snuffed it in a dangerous number of city dwellers. First of all, the rural and small community people who move to a large, strange, and hostile or indifferent city can't transplant the sense they had; and, secondly, the influx of strangers into the major cities, particularly because many are southern blacks, alters the city's identity for the natives and long-time residents. The population flux has been a deterrent to city unity; it will continue to be that unless we cleverly can turn it to everyone's advantage.

I like the idea of city creators turning population flux to their advantage. I like it not merely because it turns tables on a hitherto uncontrolled, disruptive force but also because modern urban taste for civic virtues runs toward the dynamic and active side. There are, you know, bucolic civic virtues; among them are harmony, peace, quiet, calmness, and equilibrium. These are fine if you want to live in nice, neighborly small towns; personally, I left that a long time ago because one of the civic vices that goes along with the bucolic civic virtues is bucolic boredom. Nothing happens. And in small towns the sign that all is well is that it looks as if nothing will continue to happen. Small towns are a drag. So is the countryside. Good cities are dynamic.

Anonymity is another prized value a city offers its inhabitants that is unobtainable in small communities. Anonymity provides privacy, which is a form of freedom. As the mediaeval saying has it: Stadtluft macht frei! City air makes men free! No authored city can win acceptance today if it is a cramped collection of small towns because most people are not willing to give up the freedom anonymity brings; consequently, the sense of community for which I am striving cannot be an imitation of the communal feeling small towns (or communes or tribes) foster.

Small town community sense depends upon acquaintance with a large segment of its population; you feel neighborly; you read the obituary notices with concern; your local newspaper features silver and golden wedding anniversaries; paternalism is rife; you contribute to the shudder of disapproval that races through the town when one of its unmarried women is impregnated.

I definitely want to forestall the reader's inference that because I've touted the neighborhoods I'm in favor of bucolic virtues. I am not advocating exclusive weeviling into neighborhoods as people weevil into small towns; that would, in effect, be a denial of the city, and would frustrate the desire for anonymity. I'm not denying the city, I'm promoting it. What I advocate is the commerce between neighborhoods that would take advantage of and preserve their diversity.

City virtues and emotions, unlike those of small towns, are unbucolic. They gyrate out of animation, excitement, crisis, irritation, conflict, imbalance, competition, beginnings; it would be absurd to discuss a sense of the city without acknowledging its dynamic nature. The sense of community appropriate to the city inhabitant is not a bucolic sense of neighborly, harmonious familiarity; what is appropriate is a dynamic sense of power that preserves privacy.

In summary, I have maintained that none of our institutions have fulfilled their responsibilities for nurturing the civic emotions that would contribute to our sense of well-being. I have argued that the sense of community is a complex emotion that is stable and durable enough to be a significant ingredient of a sense of well-being and that it would be aroused only by a cooperative, unified city. The sense of community is the antithesis of alienation and the emotions that it fosters. Further, the sense of community should not attempt to be an imitation of a small town feeling; modern civic emotions are more dynamic and exciting than that.

This dynamic sense of community I have emphasized is not a "spectator" feeling; it is a feeling aroused only as a result of our being able to move something, of having the power to grapple with conflict and to resolve it. The feeling of dynamism accompanies action that can get results. This means that citizens must be provided with power to overcome divisions and achieve unity. This suggests that the function of a city's essential, potential parts, its neighborhoods, is to provide its citizens with power; I discuss this in the chapter after next and try to show how what I call moral power promotes understanding, the relation I advocate for unifying neighborhoods into a city.

City authors and artists face a similar task. Each has to organize material into an integrated whole, which, when its several constituents are experienced, yields a sense of the whole; in the case of a city, we want it to yield a sense of community. This suggests that the city should be conceived by us as a work of art. Unlike other works of art, it would not just be hung on the wall, or performed for spectators at leisure, or made part of a historical collection; it would be a live-in work of art; thus, it must be designed to integrate the emotions of action with the contemplative emotions. The sense of well-being may be at bottom an aesthetic sense of life; and the sense of community may be an aesthetic sense of civic life.

I remind you here of remarks I made in Chapter 2 when commenting on the flow chart. There I distinguished between means-functional and end-functional entities, and said that a city as a work of art is end-functional. I also said there that the function of a city is to create unified persons, and I have said since then that it should realize the nesting relation in order to carry out its function. This involves an apparent paradox because a city such as I advocate does not exist in reality until the nesting relation is realized, which occurs only after each component in the person-family-neighborhood-city series has been unified. Since the person's unity may be achieved simultaneously with the city's, certainly not before, as I have shown, one may, then, well ask how it is possible for a city to unify persons.

I say this is an "apparent" paradox because it appears to run counter to our conventional notion of a functional entity, where this is a notion of a means-functional entity. A paint brush, to use another example, is an instrument, a means to help the artist achieve his end of making a painting. The brush as a means exists prior to its functioning. This, however, is not true of the painting. The painting is the end, not an instrument to be used to make something else. It comes into existence at the point when it yields the feeling the painter wanted; unlike the brush, the painting did not exist prior to its functioning; its existence and functioning occurred simultaneously. The same is true for a city; like a painting, it is an end, not an instrument; it comes into existence when the nesting relation is realized and that cannot occur until unified persons come into existence. That is the time when the sense of community, the aesthetic response to the city, also occurs. So, the city functions like other works of art; it is end-functional.

I recommended earlier that we should use the nesting relation as our guide to the structure of the city we are to create. This is a structure possessed by a novel, another work of art; we used the novel as an example in explaining the nesting relation. In the remainder of this chapter, I examine the demands that the nesting relation makes on any candidate for the relation that would unify neighborhoods into a city of the kind we want. This is the final preparation for the actual discussion of the unification of the city, which I begin in the next chapter (The Embrace of Understanding).

Recall that the nesting relation is a complex relation that consists of four relations—serial, disonion, differential, and mutuality. I shall discuss them in that order.

A serial gap between the nuclear family and the city is too large. Families, if we take our evidence from suburbia, do not form practical parts of a city. Nuclear families have failed to coalesce across their grassy moats despite the advertisers' alluring promise of a "garden community." Communal swimming pools do not seem equal to the job.

Between the family and the city, then, we need other entities that will have families for parts and which entities will, in turn, be part of a city. That is why in planning the serial property of our authored city's nesting relation we need to insert neighborhoods between families and the city.

There is a great deal of conceptual confusion about neighborhoods that should alert us to the need for more thinking about them than I do here. My argument goes through, I believe, even though I don't clarify the confusion; but I do acknowledge that I am leaping over a topic I would have to deal with in more detail were I to claim that my essay on cities is complete. Jane Jacobs is good on neighborhoods (*The Death and Life of Great American Cities*).

The literature on neighborhoods reveals that they are sometimes identified with a block, or with a shopping district, or with an elementary school district, or with an area defined by an historical building and development period, or with an ethnic occupancy area, or by major transportation boundaries, or by political division, or by income levels, or shared social values, or by neighborhood council boundary decisions. This diversity of neighborhood criteria reveals, perhaps, the source of much civic disunity because many of these criteria may be either uncoordinated or at cross purposes with one another. The decision about where to build a new school may nullify the effects of a new shopping center, for example.

The diversity of criteria of neighborhood identity may also force us to acknowledge that between the family and the city there should be other entities plugged into our serial order. Perhaps we ought to make the order, for example, person-family-block-neighborhood-servicehood-city. This would not alter the basic structure of the nesting relation but only plug more stages into it.

Guided by the nesting relation structure, we recognize, as authors of cities, that the differential property dictates that the relations which unify family parts into one neighborhood are different from those that unify neighborhood parts into one city. For example, if ideally neighborhoods were identified on the basis of shared life-styles and social values, they would basically be unified because their families share neighborhood values. Cities, by contrast, could not be so unified because basically the neighborhoods would not share those values with each other.

If we were to adopt shared sets of values as the criterion by which to define the boundaries of neighborhoods, it follows that the existence of numerous diverse sets of values—which is the case in large cities—would lead to the creation of a multiplicity of neighborhoods. The recent revival of pride in ethnic cultures and a growing wish to live in proximity to cultural brothers and sisters makes this neighborhood definition a feasible possibility. This diverse multiplicity is precisely the anti-bucolic source of a dynamic sense of community —providing we can discover a relation to unify neighborhoods without destroying their diversity. If we can discover such a relation, then we have a justifiable hope of creating a dynamic sense of community.

In searching for a unifying relation for neighborhoods that encourages and nurtures a dynamic sense of community, we can isolate another of its contextual features by observing the demands the mutuality property of the nesting relation makes on it. The mutuality property holds between the parts and the whole of which they are a part, and it has two aspects: First, the nature of the parts affects the nature of the whole, and, secondly, the conception of the whole in the creator's mind guides him in constructing and relating the parts. The first aspect of the mutuality property holds because there can be no complex whole without parts; the whole simply is the parts unified into a new something we call the "whole." There is no city over and above the neighborhoods unified.

One can, however, conceive of a non-existent whole with non-existent parts because we can, as we discovered in the fourth chapter, conceive of potential parts. This makes the second aspect of the mutuality property possible. Let us watch it work its influence: My conception of the city will influence the choice of relation that I recommend we use to unify neighborhood parts in creating our city; this follows from the view that there is no city over and above the neighborhood parts unified; and whatever response we want the city to arouse is the response that the neighborhoods unified must arouse.

I have argued that the city should arouse a dynamic sense of community. Since there is no dynamism without power, no one may feel a dynamic sense of community without having a sense of power. Our search will focus, therefore, under the influence of the mutuality property, on a relation between neighborhoods that, while it unifies them and preserves their diversity, arms the inhabitants with power.

In summary, the relation proposed to unify neighborhoods must be able to accommodate such additions as block and servicehood to the person-family-neighborhood-city series; it must be capable of unifying neighborhoods without erasing their diversity; it needs only to be fit for unifying neighborhoods into a city and does not have to account for unifying families into neighborhoods; and it should be a relation capable of providing persons in neighborhoods with power.

While we are poised on the lip of considering a power-giving relation that unifies neighborhoods, it would be wise to introduce some salutary realism into this discussion by considering the power that divides.

Violence erupts from the attempt to use physical power to suppress and resist what is different and/or disliked. Using physical power is a crude method of trying to unify the diverse; victory does not always bring unification. A painfully immediate and familiar example dramatizes this truism: Think of suppressed minority riots and rebellion in our cities, or prosecuted perpetrators of terrorist bombings. Violent conflict is a vivid revelation that a sense of community does *not* exist.

Riots, rebellion, and bombings are often known, as presently, to have no chance of overthrowing the suppressing party. Then what is the point of rioting and rebelling? Listen: It is a desperate attempt to communicate the distress of outlawed diversity; it is a searing appeal for equal power and participation in determining the nature of a community.

Riots and bombs are a sign of failure. They signal the utter failure of the oppressive segment of our society. They signal the failure of white middle and upper classes to unite with the poor and the minorities, with a failure to solve their own alienation.

I hope you feel a proper sense of urgency about creating a sense of community. You must realize that the profound civic crisis of our time erupts from our failure to solve the problem of the One and the Many. Philosophical problems aren't remote, abstract issues confined to a small cadre of isolated thinkers; they are problems that freight the souls of all of us.

In the last few chapters, I have outlined the skeletal structure of our proposed city by analyzing the nesting relation, identified the emotional pay-off of civic unity as a dynamic sense of community, discussed the reason why the unity of society (outer correlatents) is a condition for the unity of persons (inner correlatents), and specified the price we pay for not unifying by setting out the emotional chaos wrought by Marbleman alienation.

Our next step is to concentrate on the search for a relation that will unify neighborhoods into a city; this is to concentrate on only a part of what is required to create a unified city, as a moment's reflection on the various differential stages of the series in the nesting relation will confirm. But concinnation must start somewhere.

11 THE EMBRACE OF UNDERSTANDING

No, Straynger, Luv is not enuffe.
—FANEBIUS PERLYNG

The unifying relation between neighborhoods is a form of understanding, what I call "social understanding." Social understanding requires taking others' points of view to some degree.

❀   ❀   ❀

THE JUDEO-CHRISTIAN view of man has dominated United States thought. In this view, man, since the Fall in the Garden of Eden, has inherited his sin from Adam. The rest of man's days on earth were to be spent wrestling with the wrong which man's bodily desires and emotions tempt him to do. This view has dominated our thought about the proper role of government. That role is seen as primarily negative and regulatory: Government is to furnish no control measures over those Adamic desires beyond those which police power provides.

I have already commented on the two major exceptions to negative government control. Schools as presently supported provide positive controls and channels, mainly for the youth; and social services are desperate efforts to stitch up the revealing rents in our rotting social fabric. These attempts at positive action are, respectively, insufficient and temporary expedients.

The United States is a social pig sty for a lot of people. Civil rights legislation was conceived as a cleaning up operation; it was an attempt to legislate against the filth of prejudice. This political, police power solution has failed miserably. Negative, inhibitory solutions to racism are not enough. It is far better to reorient people's harmful attitudes than to provide punishments for actions prompted by them. Government must help provide a positive means of channeling the emotions that set men against each other, that divide them rather than unify them, that force some to rebel and resort to violence, that balloon into prejudicial hate and disdain. Failure to take positive measures will open the road to escalated police power legislation that will offer no more long term protection than an umbrella in a hurricane.

Cities are more interesting if their neighborhood patterns exhibit cultural diversity. Such existing diversity now tends to divide the city. The moral function of Government is to provide a positive means for unifying culturally diverse neighborhoods into a city. It must do it in a way which preserves diversity, for, as I said in the previous chapter, social unity *via* conformity is an outmoded, unacceptable, small town, bucolic solution unfit for modern city air.

It is not contradictory to suppose that what is diverse may be unified. Reflections on the novel show that it is not. Consider some features about the relations of chapters to each other. First, the chapters are *different*, and, so, diverse. Yet they unify into a novel. Secondly, they are *additive*; each chapter adds something to the other chapters without negating them. Thirdly, more than being additive, for each short story adds to a collection of short stories, they *complement* each other. One chapter may show a conflict between two persons while another tells of its resolution. Fourthly, unless deliberately flouted for special reasons, the sentences in the chapters may be logically *consistent* with each other.

Chapters aren't neighborhoods nor are novels cities, so the relations that unify chapters into novels aren't identical to those that unify neighborhoods into cities. But we can take the more abstract features of the novel's unifying relation such as the four I mentioned—difference, additivity, complementarity and consistency—as clues to a unifying relation appropriate to diverse neighborhoods.

Neighborhoods are human units. Men nest in them. The appropriate relation unifying the many neighborhoods will be one which is suited to humans, remembering that we are dealing with creatures who prize transcendental freedom, and remembering that this freedom flows from taking self-correcting thought.

You may be ahead of me. Reminding you of the source of our freedom may have neoned to you that our unifying relation lies in the realm of thought. That is the view I will take. I suggest that our unifying relation is a form of understanding.

The use of the word "understanding" which I am after is instanced in the sentence "He is an understanding person." To be understanding in this sense is to understand people, not things or theories, and requires knowing not only facts about them and their situations but also appreciating the accompanying feelings, attitudes, and interests which affect their judgments and their actions. If you have been cheated by some one, your stance toward him is not fully expressed by the purely factual statement "X cheated me." You also feel resentment, perhaps betrayal, disappointment if you've trusted him, wariness of any further dealings with him, probably anger as well. These feelings and attitudes influence your future relations with and actions toward the cheater. You may cease being his friend; you may tell others of what he has done and so cut him off from other of his friends; or you may let the air out of his car tires.

In saying that understanding is the relation that unifies neighborhoods into cities, I am, of course, saying something that I believe I can defend. That defense will take up most of what comes next in this chapter. On the other hand, if I said that understanding is the *only* relation between neighborhoods which can contribute to city unity, I would be guilty of an indefensible oversimplification, as guilty as if I said that only understanding and cooperation cement families into neighborhoods, and as guilty as if I said that only understanding, cooperation, and love bind persons into families. The binding relations that exist between persons are incredibly numerous. I am concentrating on understanding in this essay because I believe it is the unifying relation that yields a sense of city community, just as understanding and cooperation yield a sense of neighborhoods, and understanding, cooperation, and love yield a sense of family.

A complete study of the binding relations between persons would be exceedingly larger than this essay. If it were carried out in the spirit of this essay, it would be a complete ethic. A complete ethic would be a set of recommended ways that human bodies should be related to each other so that all the healthy needs of those bodies, biological, psychological, and social, would be equitably and maximally satisfied. Such an ethic would recommend the inner correlatents of which persons should be composed, would provide a description of them as ideals to be attained, and would recommend an organization of society that would enable persons to realize their ideal selves. In this essay, I confine myself mainly to a city ethic, hence to a description of an ideal city and an ideal citizen relatent.

To help communicate my conception of social understanding, hearken back to my notion of a person.

A person, I said, is a collection of inner correlatents. These correlatents, and, so, the person, come into being when a human body enters into certain relations with another human

body or socially united bodies such as families and neighborhoods. Up to this point, I have discussed relatents as if they
were a purely factual matter; however, one of the ways we
talk about persons prompts me to point out that the concept
of a relatent is as much a moral as it is a factual concept. The
moral aspect of relatents is central to our moral talk about
persons, as when we say of them that they are "good parents"
or "bad bosses." To comprehend how we are able to judge
persons' moral character, to realize what it means to say some
one is "good" or "bad," we must grasp the moral nature of
relatents.

One concept of mother is defined purely factually: Maud
is a mother if Maud had intercourse, conceived and gave birth
to a child. Another concept of mother is defined morally: A
mother is a woman who cares for a child by feeding, fondling,
diapering, loving it, etc. "Mother" names two different relatents which we might label "factual-mother" and "moral-
mother."

"Moral-mother" is an ideal relatent. It defines a good mother; it specifies what relations should obtain between two bodies if we are to say that one of them is a person whose collection
of inner correlatents contains the moral-mother relatent. Our
short way of saying that such relations obtain is to say "X is a
good mother." We also have a short way of denying the existence of such relations: "X is a bad mother." This shows us
that "bad" is a form of moral negation; it denies the presence
of the moral-mother relatent in X's person.

Though I have distinguished factual- from moral-relatents,
reflections on blame reveal that the two are intimately con-
nected. We do not blame everyone for lacking some moral
relatent or other; we do not blame the virgin because her
person does not include a moral-mother relatent. We do not
blame her as we might blame the woman who gave birth to
a child. The virgin is not blameworthy because she is not a
factual-mother. A body that becomes pregnant and gives birth

adds to her person a factual-mother inner correlatent; in doing so, she becomes obliged to fulfill the ideals of moral-motherhood as well, lodging in others' minds the demand that she undertake to act morally in order to actualize that ideal inner correlatent. Criticism of her moral-motherhood becomes relevant because of the acts that made her a factual-mother. She is (a) "bad" in (b) a certain respect, namely, motherhood. We can say she is bad because we could demand of her that she assume the duties and obligations of moral-motherhood, but she did not do so. In general, except under extenuating circumstances, the presence of a factual-relatent in a person obligates the person to actualize the corresponding moral-relatent.

Similarly, the person who moves to a city and becomes a factual-citizen has the duty to become a good-citizen; the person who becomes a factual-employee has the duty to become a good-employee, just as the factual-employer has the duty to become a good-employer.

We do not fully comprehend persons when we consider their factual-relatents alone; we must also consider their moral-relatents, for to think of persons is to think of them as moral beings, as good and bad, and this necessitates considering the presence and absence of the appropriate moral-relatents in the collections of inner correlatents comprising them. Moral-relatents are artifacts; they are the product of taking thought. One does not have to take thought to be a factual-son; it is something that happens to you. You do, however, have to take thought both for the creation and knowledge of the moral-son relatent and take self-correcting thought in order to be a good son. In taking self-correcting thought you become transcendent.

A perfectly good person would possess a moral-relatent for every factual-relatent he possesses; the saint, by taking on obligations beyond those imposed by his constituent factual-relatents, would possess more. The ideal person is the goal for which transcendent beings should strive; the ideal person is the perfect artificial man, a product of thoughtful reflection about the kind of relations which a body ought to have to other bodies if the best possible person and society are to be created.

Alas! We are neither perfectly good nor do we have a clear, full characterization of the ideal person. We are bad to the extent that we possess some factual-relatents whose corresponding moral-relatents we lack. Sometimes this is so because our bodies' emotions detrack us on the run for perfection as defined by our ideal, moral-relatents; and sometimes this is so because we lack a clear formulation of the ideals and don't know which way to run.

This addition of moral relatents gives us a fuller notion of persons and will help us get a better grasp of the concept of understanding, to which I now return.

To understand another person requires taking his point of view; you understand him when you have taken his point of view.

What is it you've taken when you've taken his point of view? How do you take someone's point of view?

These questions can't be answered satisfactorily until we have a good analysis of the concept "point of view." The best way of getting into the concept is to discover the factors which make one point of view different from another. I suggest there are at least three such factors: Factual knowledge, immanent emotions, and moral-relatents. A difference in any one or more of them produces a different viewpoint.

"Point of view" interpreted literally designates a place from which to see something. If two people are in different places, what they see is different. One person might accuse Bruno of striking another without provocation while some one else would not because from his point of view he saw that Bruno was attacked by the man and struck in self-defense.

The literal meaning of "point of view" has been extended in

our language so that it includes all factual knowledge, not just that knowledge acquired because you were visually viewing something from a particular vantage point. This means, for instance, that a master chef has a point of view of scallops different from that of the young bride. Factual knowledge, then, is one of the factors which contributes to a point of view.

Our camera zooms in on two lions: Leo, gorged to his gullet, is fighting with Leonard over a piece of meat. We have front row seats: Othello is smothering Desdemona. We open the newspaper: There is a picture of a white man casting the first stone at a civil rights demonstrator, a venomous yell frozen on his face. Each of these incidents contains a conscious being exhibiting an interest different from another's. Those interests are so possessing and their accompanying emotions are so heightened that they lead the actors to perform an extreme act that is harmful to another.

We understand why those beings acted as they did because we can explain their actions; their actions are caused by their interests and emotions. We are dealing with the order of nature here. We are dealing with conscious beings in their immanent state. They are in the grip of emotional states uncontrolled and uncorrected by thought or artifice.

Leo has his point of view; he wants that meat despite his being gorged. Leonard does too. But if Leonard had Leo's interest and emotional point of view, he wouldn't fight Leo for the meat; he would be interested only in Leo's getting the meat. If Leonard always had someone else's emotional point of view and never one of his own, Leonard would starve. Neither pure self-interest—always taking only your own emotional point of view—nor pure other-interest—taking only someone else's emotional point of view—are satisfactory points of view for man. We are well advised to take thought and create another, mediate point of view, namely, a social point of view.

The social point of view lies outside any one emotional point of view; to construct it requires considering all emotional points of view and ideally all factual points of view. This social point of view when fully stated is an ethic. For each person it provides a set of ideal, moral-relatents. These moral-relatents are each person's allotment of the artificially created social viewpoint; they are his viewpoint insofar as he is transcendent. This viewpoint provides standards with which to transcend his own interests and emotions and provides duties and obligations which guide his action.

A difference of viewpoint arises not only when two persons' facts or emotions are at odds but also when their conceptions of a moral-relatent differ. Not everyone has the same idea of what it is to be an ideal mother. One person might criticize a mother for not breastfeeding her child while another is indifferent.

Each moral-relatent is a facet of some projected social point of view. These facets don't always neatly fit. Antigone was victimized because two of hers didn't. From the point of view of being a good citizen she should obey Creon, her king, who forbade her to bury her brother, Polyneices, and from the point of view of being a good religious person she should bury Polyneices. She died following the obligations of religion and violating the obligations of a citizen.

The moral-relatent viewpoints, being artificial creations, must be learnt by children. In learning them and assuming those points of view, the children acquire accompanying feelings and emotions, which, unlike the immanent emotions which define the emotional point of view, are under self-corrected control; they are under the control of the moral-relatent viewpoints. Examples of such moral feelings and emotions are outrage, righteousness, decency, guilt, tolerance, love, restraint, violation, loyalty, honesty, kindness, fortitude, good-will, and benevolence. The moral feelings and emotions are under rational control for they arise only after the standards inherent in taking a moral-relatent point of view have been applied; the standards also provide a basis for self-correction of our initial emotional responses and for justification. For example, you feel guilty only because you recognize that you did something wrong; you feel outraged with someone because they did you a wrong; you feel righteous because what you did was in accord with your moral standards; you feel a strong sense of fortitude because you are buoyed up by the rightness of your cause. Moral emotions are possible because we can transcend a circumscribed, crude, immanent, animal-like point of view. In transcending, we progress toward a social point of view.

To understand another, thus, sometimes requires looking at the world through the grid structured by his moral-relatent viewpoints. By adopting his grid even temporarily, we understand the basis for his actions, convictions, and justifications, and for his moral feelings and emotions.

Understanding another, then, requires taking his point of view. At the coolest it is to know one or more of three ingredients: It is to know the facts on which he based his judgment and actions; and/or it is to know the immanent interests and emotions which explain his judgment and actions; and/or it is to know the artificial moral-relatents he used to correct his immanent interests and emotions and to justify his judgments, actions, and moral feelings.

The hottest degree to which we can take some one else's viewpoint would be one which includes feeling with the same intensity the same emotions, immanent and moral, which the other feels *in addition* to knowing the three ingredients of his point of view. Naturally, there are varying degrees of heat with which we may take another's viewpoint. It would be easier for most Blacks to take the viewpoint of revolutionary Blacks than it would be for most Whites; and among those who could take that viewpoint, the degree to which a Black person took it would tend to be hotter than the degree to which a White person did. It requires less imagination for the

Black than for the White, since he is more likely to know more of the facts known to the rebels; he is more likely to have the same immanent interests and to have felt the same immanent emotions; and he is more likely to share their moral-relatents.

For the White person to take the Black's viewpoint would call for a strong exercise of his imagination, especially because it would require his seeing himself from their viewpoint—one likely to pass harsh moral judgment on him. We are frequently reluctant to condemn ourselves, and, because taking a viewpoint makes the judgments from that viewpoint plausible, we prefer to avoid adopting the Black person's condemnatory viewpoint. Whites have the same difficulty in adopting a Black point of view that David had in adopting Uriah's. It took a parable of Nathan's to covertly slip David into Uriah's viewpoint.

How Nathan confronted David with a parable is told in II Samuel, Ch. 12, 1–7. David had got Bathsheba with child; her husband, Uriah, was now a nuisance to David, so David arranged that Uriah should be placed in the forefront of the most dangerous sector of the battle for Rabbah, expecting that Uriah would be killed. He was killed. The Lord, being displeased, sent Nathan to David, and Nathan told David about the rich man and the poor man. The rich man had many flocks, the poor man had a single little ewe lamb. When a traveler came to visit the rich man, he killed the poor man's lamb to feed the traveler. At this point in the telling, David hotly assumed the poor man's viewpoint.

> And David's anger was greatly kindled against the man; and he said to Nathan, As the Lord liveth, the man that hath done this thing shall surely die.
> And he shall restore the lamb fourfold, because he did this thing, and because he had not pity.
> And Nathan said to David, Thou art the man.

David, the king, was to Uriah as the rich man was to the poor man. David was unable to take Uriah's viewpoint, for David would have had to condemn himself with all the convictions and righteousness which Uriah's viewpoint would provide. David was able, however, not being personally involved in the rich man-poor man story, to adopt the poor man's viewpoint. In taking that viewpoint, David acquired all the convictions and righteousness that were needed to judge and act justly against himself.

The moral importance of understanding that part of another's viewpoint from which he judges and acts toward us should be too obvious to you to need my harangues. It's pretty obvious, also, that achieving this kind of understanding will require more than a few parables. In Chapter 12, I will suggest the means by which such understanding can be nurtured.

We have now got some purchase on what it means to understand another person. We can use this purchase to boost ourselves to the next plane from whence I can show you why understanding is the relation that can unify Many neighborhoods into One city.

Earlier in this chapter, I isolated four abstract features about the unity of a novel—chapter differences, their additivity, complementarity, and consistency. These four features of unified chapters are also the features of understanding, the relation I suggest may be used to unify neighborhoods into a city.

First, neighborhoods differ from each other as do chapters. And as different chapters can be parts of a single novel, so can the different viewpoints of neighborhoods be accommodated in a single understanding. Given the facts and a strong imagination or proper imaginative aid, you are perfectly capable of understanding the people in diverse neighborhoods.

Secondly, understanding one neighborhood does not negate your understanding of another neighborhood. Understanding is additive; each time you come to understand another neighborhood, your understanding cumulates.

Thirdly, our understanding of the people in one neighborhood receives complementary support from our understanding of the people in another neighborhood. Complementary reinforcement of one understanding by another is familiar to people who read histories of man's civilizations. One of the most striking things we learn to appreciate about man from these histories is his exceeding variability. Another thing we learn to appreciate is that the variations are not sealed off from one other. The stiff, profile sculpture of ancient Egypt was a departure point for the ancient Greek sculptors who amplified and developed what they inherited. Your understanding of the ancient Greeks is complemented if you understand ancient Egyptian influence on them. Our understanding of Man, the human creature, is a tissue of understanding the variations on the human theme which complement each other. Part of that tissue is the complementary understandings of co-existing neighborhood variations.

Though neighborhood variations may be less pronounced than the variations of civilizations, they are not different in kind. Travel is fascinating and important to us because one of its chief rewards is complementary understanding. Observing the formal decorum of married couples in another country can tutor a fresh perception and appreciation of the more relaxed, casual demeanor of our own marriage partners.

Consistency, the fourth abstract feature, is not automatically achieved when we come to understand others. I may have succeeded in grasping another's point of view; the fact that his point of view and mine are both contained in my understanding does not guarantee that they are consistent; though I understand why he judged or acted as he did, that understanding does not imply that I agree with his judgment, or would have acted as he did were I in his situation.

The fact that I may ingest into my personal understanding several conflicting points of view renders personal understanding unsuitable to unify a diverse city. City unity depends upon transcending personal understanding and achieving a socially shared understanding. This shared, consistent understanding is constructed by citizens who excise the conflicting elements in their viewpoints. Failure to so employ their self-correcting, intellectual artifice dooms their city to factual, emotional, and moral schizophrenia, while successful self-correction will lead to the construction of a single, shared, consistent point of view that will replace our individual or class points of view. As I said in Chapter 2, a social point of view, being one, unifies (one-ifies) a city's parts.

Achieving complete social understanding is an ideal goal beyond our practical reach. The larger the social body, the more beyond our reach it is. Three factors, the very three which compose a point of view, must be shared before complete social understanding can be realized. First, everyone must possess the same facts; secondly, our social and psychological restructuring capabilities must be sufficiently advanced to eliminate all the immanent emotions that produce irreconcilable emotional points of view; and, thirdly, citizens must have participated in enough philosophical discussions with each other to have eliminated conflicting conceptions of the moral-relatents which set forth our duties and obligations. The difficulty of the philosophical undertaking can be appreciated by anyone who has read Plato's *The Republic*, the best example in literature of the technique for guiding initially divergent conceptions of moral-relatents into similar conceptions.

Now that you have a better grasp of my point of view, you should be able to understand my passion in urging cities to become independent city-states and to understand why I asked you to give your main effort and first loyalty to your city should we fail to secede. The city, having a smaller girth than the nation, will be easier to embrace in social understanding, yet it is muscled with enough diversity to make our social understanding a splendid transcendental achievement.

12 MORAL POWER

Sire, wud hav mye facks?
Glaidly, fore you knowe much.
Sire, wud have my feelyngs?
Wyth plaisur, fore you ar faibeled fore their finenesse.
And, Sire, wud have mye ydeels?
Moste wyllyngly, fore I aspire to yor lofte.
Cum, then, Sire, and I wyll maik thee me.
—FROM "AWL POWR TO FANEBIUS"

My thesis in this chapter clusters around the motive force behind "dynamic" in "dynamic sense of community," which, I argued, is the only appropriate sense of community for a modern city. If every citizen is to have this dynamic sense, every citizen must have access to power. The power to which he must have access is one that enables him to establish the unifying relation of understanding. I call this moral power; it is the power of infusing in others an understanding of his neighborhood, the power of placing in the minds of others his neighborhood's point of view.

❦ ❦ ❦

MY CITY, San Francisco, like other major cities in the United States, is sundering. The Many is triumphing over the One. This trend cannot be reversed unless cities make it their major business to promote action which will unify their neighborhoods into One.

I have argued that when they unify, cities produce a sense of community in their inhabitants, that this sense should be a dynamic one, and that this dynamic sense of community cannot be produced until each citizen has access to power. In the last chapter, I argued that the unifying relation between neighborhoods which will preserve diversity is social understanding. The kind of power to which citizens must have equal access, then, must be one whose exercise fosters social understanding. Such a power is a civilizing power.

Most people look with moral suspicion on persons openly seeking power. This is a prudent attitude, for, should the powerseeker sedulously seek and finally find enough power to outweigh your own, you would be at his mercy, and, considering the scanty distribution of mercy and benevolence, you would be at a distinct disadvantage. Egomaniacal powerseekers have given power an undeserved bad name because their excesses have driven people to indiscriminately condemn power itself rather than the persons who misuse it. It is time someone said a good word for power, and a good word, I think, is this: Power and the even distribution of it are necessary before there can be a tolerant and just society.

Power is a means for getting someone else to do something for you, or to give you something. It is also a means of self-protection; it protects you from having to do something for someone that you don't want to do and from giving something to someone that you don't want to give. If evenly distributed, power is a two-headed arrow. If evenly distributed, power promotes respect, consideration, and tolerance of others, all of which are necessary for a just society. Power enables us to fulfill our social obligations and express our social love.

Benevolence is exercised by almost everyone sometimes toward a few. It is not exercised by everyone all the time toward everybody. That is why neither governments nor social organizations, including churches, can be run on the principle of benevolence alone. Your expectation of just behavior and a tolerant attitude from someone is much more likely to be met if you have some power which he respects than if you depend solely on his benevolence. Benevolent despots are the rare exception—and you must keep in mind that an elected legislature may play a despotic role just as well as a one-man dictatorship may.

From the rarity of benevolent despots, however, we should not conclude that power is bad and ought to be eliminated. We should conclude instead that *the uneven distribution* of power is bad, and that power in and of itself is neither good nor bad. You may use your power to get someone else to do something good or bad, or to prevent someone else from having something good or bad, and so may others.

Power takes many forms.

Some people wield power over others by means of physical threat. A big man with a pipe wrench in hand who clearly intends to use the wrench as a weapon if the course of events requires it has power.

Some people wield power by means of money. They may be able to fire an employee, refuse to give a loan or extend the due date on a promissory note; or they may bribe persons who are rendered helpless by greed.

Some people wield power by psychological means. They play upon a person's fears, superstitions, dislikes, suspicions, or ideals.

Of two persons, otherwise equally matched, the one with the most information has the most power. If I know a company is unable to pay a debt and you do not, which of us would an investor rather have for his stockbroker? Sex appeal, organizational prowess, beauty, persuasiveness, and family connections are all sources of power.

There is legislative power. Check that tax bill and the penalty for avoiding its payment. Why do you smoke your

pot clandestinely? Itching to get a few thrills from your 325
horsepower engine but afraid the patrolmen will radio ahead?
And that the judge won't be sympathetic?

When voters give their legislative power to their representatives they create an uneven distribution of power, since
the voters themselves simply do not have the power that their
supervisor, assemblyman, or senator has.

As a well programmed U. S. citizen, I'm sure you've already
hidden from this ominous truth by wrapping yourself in the
power of the ballot. Dare to face reality. Remind yourself that
the ballot is simply one small part of the complicated process
of determining who shall exercise legislative power. Otherwise, citizen, how high are you in the councils of the political
parties? How much money do you have to contribute to cam-
paigns? What are your family and business connections with
your legislators? How does all that stack up against your single
vote?

Vote power is unequal to the task of protecting everyone
against their representatives, even though the ballot is evenly
distributed. A legislature elected by the same people year
after year, acting in the interests of the majority which elected
it, soon acts despotically and unbenevolently toward the
permanent minority. Representative government functions
undespotically only when there is not a permanent minority.
A minority can avoid the dungeon of permanence and the
lash of despotism only if it is able to find allies with which it
may either coalesce into the majority or seriously threaten to
coalesce into the majority—only, that is, if it grasps or threat-
ens to grasp a hold on legislative power.

The secret, evenly distributed ballot is a form of power
provided that the voter does not belong to a permanent minority. Clearly, the even distribution of the ballot does not guarantee social justice because equal access to the vote does not
guarantee equal access to power.

I am not indulging in theoretical talk as a dear friend of the

Disunited League of Probable Minority Voters. At this point in our history, practically speaking, the United States is a sinking ship from which our cities ought to jump because an increasing number of young and minority people in this country are developing a permanent contempt for the ballot and politics. They have seen through the pretence of the ballot here, where it is the sole form of distributed power. They have observed too many permanent minorities in America, too many domestic emigrés forever beyond the pale of benevolence—the youth, the black, the farm workers, the Puerto Ricans, the coal miners, the Indians, the artists, the peace lovers, the draftables, and so on and on.

The ballot is finished here. It cannot save itself. It has destroyed itself as an instrument of social good. It has been turned into an instrument of majoritarian politicians, into a charade which only Republicans and Democrats can play, players more mindful of themselves than the minorities (other than Establishment minorities such as the oil barons, the Millionaires Club, and the tax lawyers).

The inhabitants of our cities need equal access to another kind of social power than the ballot. But the country as a whole is too large and lost to be able to offer access to this power; only cities if reconstituted along the lines laid out in this essay can offer it.

I suggest that one kind of power that will bring justice and tolerance to our city is *moral power*.

The concept of moral power is easy to grasp once you have the concept of understanding. Understanding someone, you'll recall, is to some degree taking his point of view. This, in turn, means knowing the facts he knows about something; knowing his interests, and feeling to some degree the emotions which buttress those interests; as well as knowing his moral-relatents and feeling to some degree the moral emotions which attend those moral-relatents. Being able to take someone's point of view warmly requires an act of imagination on your part.

By moral power, I mean the power of being able to give another person understanding, of being able to lodge in him yours or someone else's point of view. You exercise the ultimate form of moral power when you displace a person's point of view with another, or when, in addition to lodging in someone a different point of view, you also suspend, at least temporarily, the influence of his own.

It may help you to appreciate the high place occupied by moral power in the scale of powers if we consider David and Nathan once again. David was a king; he had armies, wealth, political allies, and the immense prerogatives of his office. Nathan had none of these, yet Nathan had power over David. David had wronged Uriah with impunity; there was no higher political power that could judge or punish David. Still, Nathan with his moral power could force David to judge and correct himself. "And David said unto Nathan, I have sinned against the Lord." If you recall my previous analysis of the parable, you will perceive that the source of Nathan's moral power lay in his skill to infuse Uriah's viewpoint into David while lulling David's own viewpoint into quiescence.

It is not difficult to understand how the ability to displace, even temporarily, a point of view gives one so much power. Your own responses, decisions, attitudes, judgments, emotions, and actions are what they are because of your point of view; modify your viewpoint and you modify your responses, decisions, attitudes, judgments, emotions, and actions.

Suppose, now, that someone were able to displace totally your point of view with his point of view, at least temporarily. What consequences would follow from that? You would have the same facts, the same interests and emotions, and the same moral-relatents and moral emotions as the other person. The consequences of that, in turn, would be that you would respond, decide, attitudinize, judge, emote, and act as he would. You would be, in short, a carbon copy of that other person.

Clearly enough, if another can infuse into you his point of

view, while anesthetizing your own, he will have control of you. This degree of control is the ultimate form of power over humans. What better way for him to settle a disagreement between yourself and him? In his favor. Here is a form of power so ultimate that the mere thought of unequal access to it pales the scrupulous.

I have taken a risk in calling this kind of power "moral power," for that name suggests that it is a power possessed only by moral men or that it can be used only for good.

Moral power is not the possession solely of good men. It is not the menace of God's angry man standing in a pulpit, pointing thunderbolts of terror at hearts and minds made doubly vulnerable by guilt and inferiority. Nor should we equate moral power with the pulse behind the psychologist's purr, ministering to the sick, the neurotic, and the mad weakened by doubt, torment, and confusion. Moral power is the possession of no special class or trained profession. It is the possession of anyone skillful enough to displace temporarily or permanently one point of view by another in some person.

Nor is moral power useful only for good. Since the evil as well as the good can use it, moral power—like other powers— may be used for base purposes as well as noble. A vengeful, underpaid employee may con the similarly disaffected to be accomplices in thefts to right the economic wrong of which they are the "victims." On being conned into a victim's point of view, the accomplices may feel perfectly justified in their thievery. Or the officers of a union or a medical society may so insistently and persuasively point out to their members the economic threat of admitting Black people into the union or more students into medical schools that the members may proceed to judge and act from their economic point of view alone, thereby restricting membership and limiting enrollment.

I have risked calling this power "moral power," despite the fact that it may be used for good or ill, because no other power is as effective in promoting understanding and, thereby, justice and tolerance. In order to show the plausibility of this claim, we shall have to consider the notion of a social point of view at greater length than we did in the previous chapter.

13 THE SOCIAL POINT OF VIEW: JUSTICE AND TOLERANCE

A rownd penny fore yor vuepoynt.
—FANEBIUS PERLYNG

Equal access to moral power creates the conditions that lead men to modify their personal points of view in favor of a social point of view, without which there cannot be a just and tolerant city.

❀　❀　❀

THERE ARE AT least as many points of view in a collection of persons as there are persons. It is highly unlikely that any two persons share all facts, interests, and moral-relatents. To the extent that persons' points of view differ, to that extent they constitute a Many. And to the extent that they are a Many to that extent they are vulnerable to conflict. And to the extent that they are vulnerable to conflict, they are to that extent liable to act at cross purposes. And if they are liable to act at cross purposes, they are likely to frustrate each other's aims. And should they wish to avoid frustration of their aims, they are to that extent justified in working to transform the Many persons into One society.

Why is it that if persons—by virtue of their different points of view—constitute a Many, they are vulnerable to conflict?

A conflict occurs when two or more persons perform contrary actions. Now, an action is something a person performs in carrying through a decision; assuming a rational actor, a decision is based on a judgment about the value of the action; hence, contrary actions are traceable to contrary judgments of value. The answer to our question, must be sought then, in the relation between Many points of view and contrary judgments of value.

I remarked earlier on the different judgments that result from different points of view when we think of viewpoints in the literal sense. A literal viewpoint is defined in terms of the spatial relations that obtain between the viewer and what is viewed. Two different sets of spatial relations produce two different appearances. Consider two persons looking at a penny; from one person's viewpoint, the penny appears round; from the other's viewpoint, it appears elliptical. These two appearances are contrary, for an appearance that is round isn't elliptical.

But someone may now ask: Yes, I realize that the penny will look different from two different viewpoints, but what is the shape of the penny itself? If one of the persons said, "The penny is round," and the other one said, "The penny is elliptical," we would have contrary judgments, and, further, contrary judgments based on contrary evidence yielded by contrary appearances. We recognize that it is useful to share common knowledge with others; however, two persons cannot share common knowledge of, for example, the penny, if they persist in their judgments based on their two points of view of the penny. The desire for common knowledge is part of what lies in back of the question about the shape of the "penny itself." That question is a request for "objective" knowledge that everyone can or should acknowledge; it is a request to transcend the parochialism of the different points of view.

Suppose someone, in his attempt to escape "contrary" parochialism, were to assert that the "penny itself" is round.

How are we to understand this claim? I suggest that such a claim—and one most of us would affirm—consists of two parts: One, there is a viewpoint from which the penny appears round; and, two, this is the favored viewpoint we must take in deciding what the shape of the "penny itself" is. The stratagem of taking a "favored" viewpoint enables us to transcend parochialism; it is a viewpoint everyone can take in principle; and, given our knowledge of spatial relations, even from the elliptical viewpoint we can predict that it would look round were we to move from the elliptical viewpoint to the favored round viewpoint. Possession of "objective," common knowledge involves, then, a decision to favor some one viewpoint or other.

It would be interesting and important, but a diversion from the main thrust of this essay, to explore the kinds of considerations that lead us to select one viewpoint as the "favored" one.

Obviously, this discussion of "penny" viewpoints is a prelude to a discussion of value judgments, the judgments that when contrary lead to conflict. By exploiting some analogous features shared by literal points of view and figurative points of view, we can clarify our understanding of how value judgments are related to figurative viewpoints.

First, where literal viewpoints are defined by spatial relations, figurative viewpoints are defined by factual knowledge, interests and immanent emotions, and ideal moral-relatents and moral emotions.

Secondly, just as different spatial viewpoints may lead to parochial contrary visual judgments, so may different figurative viewpoints lead to parochial contrary value judgments. Think of David and Uriah, again. Despite the usefulness of the penny analogy, we should be careful to skirt an oversimplification. The visual shape of a penny is fully given in observation; value properties are not so simply detected. This does not surprise the person who realizes that the complex of relations contributed to a figurative viewpoint by facts, interests, and moral-relatents is primarily intellectual rather than sensory. Thus, even when two persons agree in words that something quite ordinary is good, this complex of relations may thwart actual agreement in judgment because the goods they have in their mind's eye may be quite different. Consider two persons, John D. Gotrocks and Earnest Poorman; both of them may say that the building of a projected subway is good. However, scrutiny of their reasons reveals different viewpoints that yield different goods. Poorman thinks a subway is good because he works downtown and the subway will get him to work more cheaply and faster than driving does; he plans to ride the subway. Gotrocks, on the other viewpoint, is driven to his executive suite in the financial district by his chauffeur; he thinks a subway is good because it will take Poorman's Volkswagen and other obstacles off the street and allow him to be driven to work in an unharried fashion. The goodness of the subway is quite different for them.

Thirdly, just as it is useful to share common factual knowledge, it is useful to share common value judgments; we are not led into frustrating conflicts if we have common value judgments on which to base the decisions that lead to our actions.

Fourthly, in the search for common judgments and common goods that provide the escape route from a radical parochialism, the history of thought is studded with well-meaning, earnest attempts to chart the course of objectivity for values. I am suggesting that "objectivity" is to be obtained in value judgments in the same way that it is obtained in visual judgments, namely, by constructing a favored point of view— what I call a social point of view.

Once again, it would be interesting and important, but part of an expansion beyond a prolegomenon were we to explore the kinds of considerations that guide us in constructing a "favored" viewpoint. Further—and this is important—the actual construction and selection of a favored viewpoint should be made in concert only by the persons who belong to the society in search of a social point of view.

In order to attain One Society, the Many persons with their Many points of view must achieve, then, a social point of view, a point of view which ideally they all share, and which, being shared, enables them to act in cooperative rather than conflicting and frustrating ways. It would be a monstrous society, however, if it adopted a social point of view governing all aspects of life, thereby erasing all differences. This would wipe out people's individuality, for everyone's point of view would then be identical in all respects. This commitment to a total social point of view would be, in a word, totalitarianism.

I have already argued for unity with diversity as the proper end of a city. In committing ourselves to this combination, we assume the burden—perhaps the heaviest we must tote while creating our new city—of drawing the line between what we can afford to leave in the country of the diverse Many and what we would be advised to shepherd into the embrace of the One. It is not difficult to say in the general and abstract what the optimum spread of a social point of view should be: We must share as much and no more of a social point of view as is necessary to attain and share equally the most good, social and personal, with the least conflict. Any society that shares that amount of a social point of view I shall call a just society.

I would reject as totally misguided any criticism of this essay based on the fact that I do not now go on to draw the boundary of a social point of view in specific and concrete detail, nor that I do not now go on to identify some figurative viewpoint as the "favored," social point of view. I would, indeed, have overstepped my proper bounds, and so would anyone else, if I, or he, were to do so. That line can only be drawn, as I shall argue in the last chapter, by a dialectical process involving all the persons in a society. Drawing the line and creating a just city is the responsibility of all of us. A viewpoint should be freely chosen, not imposed. What I do want to show here is that to create a just city, all persons in a city, striving for a social point of view, must have equal access to moral power. Showing why that is true occupies me in the rest of this chapter.

Prior to welding the last link in my argument that equal access to moral power is a necessary condition for the creation of a just city, I need to add some remarks about the tandem civil virtues—justice and tolerance.

Men demand justice that they may correct or avoid intolerable injustice to themselves. That may not be the only reason they demand justice, but, because it is one of the pervasive ones we are justified in trying to determine the conditions essential to justice by getting beneath the surface of men's reactions to injustice.

When men believe they have been unjustly judged, treated, or punished, they do so from their own point of view; consequently, the injustice is seen from the factual, interest, and/or moral-relatent facets of their viewpoint.

When men believe from a factual point of view that they have been done an injustice, they believe that someone judged them or acted against them on the basis of misinformation; they believe, for example that had the jury known all the true facts that they themselves know, they would not have been judged guilty. Factual injustice is avoidable if honest men share the same facts. The search for the same facts by the same method is a search for the truth. Truth is a social virtue, acquiring its social value because it is a necessary means to achieving a common factual point of view, and, so, is a necessary social tool in avoiding injustice.

Factual tolerance, factual justice's tandem virtue, is keeping an open minded attitude toward other persons' claims to know the true facts and a modest scepticism about one's own claims.

When we believe from an interest point of view that we have been done an injustice, we believe that the other person has given undue weight to his own interests and insufficient weight to ours. The seller who cheats the buyer is unduly interested in his own profit and insufficiently interested in the purchaser's interest in receiving full value for his money. Justice requires that we recognize that others' interests and values have *prima facie* as much claim to existence and fulfillment as ours. The prime responsibility of legislators and judges is to pass such laws and to so administer them that there is an equitable balance of satisfaction and fulfillment.

Interest tolerance, interest justice's tandem virtue, is the generous attitude that nourishes our recognition that others' interests should not be frustrated simply because they are not ours. Other things being equal, your tolerance of another's interests should equal the commitment to your own. Interest tolerance is life-blood to individual values, the mainstay of the diverse, and the bane of conformity.

To oppose tolerating others' interests implies either that you are selfish or that you hold a self-contradictory position. If you are selfish, the good of others is not among your interests; if, however, the good of others *is* one of your interests but you also believe that you should never forward someone else's interests if it will retard your own, including your own interest in the fulfillment of others' interests, then you hold a self-contradictory position. To avoid being selfish or self-contradictory, you must hold that the fulfillment of the interests of others is good and is not destructive of the fulfillment of your own interests.

When we believe from a moral-relatent point of view that we have been done an injustice, we believe that someone has prevented us from being as good a person as we want or feel obligated to be. They have cancelled the tickets for our transcendental flight.

Men believe that a society which, for example, denies them

an opportunity to earn enough money to fulfill their parental obligations is an unjust society. Parents who want to create parental moral-relatents to match their factual-relatents want to feed, clothe, comfort, and educate their children. We cannot be just, moral-relatently, unless we give others the freedom and/or opportunity to be moral men.

You have moral-relatent tolerance, moral-relatent justice's tandem virtue, if the idea of the existence of another, different, and non-conflicting kind of moral person does not offend you. You have moral-relatent tolerance if you see a person composed of other and different moral-relatents as complementary rather than as threatening to your own person. For example, that another person might choose to be a homosexual is offensive to many; they have no moral-relatent tolerance because they do not understand that persons might find a different satisfactory route to love and companionship. Homosexuality is a complementary route because it is a route to the same goals as heterosexuality—love and companionship —and does not diminish those who do not choose that route.

In summary, justice for yourself requires at a minimum that persons be truthful, that they recognize that your interests have as much right to fulfillment as their own—providing neither are destructive—and that they secure you the freedom and opportunity to become a moral person. Tolerance, justice's tandem virtue, extends factual credibility to others, generously proffers fulfillment of their interests, and respects the sanctity of their moral hopes and efforts.

A just society, then, is one in which men hold in common and live in accordance with a social point of view of an appropriate spread. That society will be tolerant as well if its citizens tolerate everything except what is unjust, that is, everything except what is false, selfish, or castrating.

Given that personal points of view differ to some degree, a social point of view can be created only if those personal points of view are modified sufficiently on a set of mutually converg-

ing lines. Those lines will keep their mutually convergent direction only if all the citizens have an equal share of power.
An unequal distribution of power will unbalance the direction
and shift them toward those with the most power. The result
of this shift would not be a social point of view but the impo-
sition of the personal or class point of view of those in power.

Rhetorically, soft historical Christianity has relied chiefly
upon benevolence to converge the lines. This has tipped its
notion of tolerance toward identification with a patronizing
attitude: Out of the charitableness of my heart I give you your
factual, interest, and moral due. Soft Christianity's excess is
sanctimoniousness. Its heavy reliance on benevolence and love
is unrealistic and its sanctimoniousness is a deadly sin—and
bore. Christ was not a soft Christian; He did not eschew power. To the unsophisticated, He appeared to eschew power because He seldom used physical power, but no one's reported
history contains a higher proportion of space devoted to tales
about the use of moral power than Christ's. Parables were His
stock in trade, and parables, as we saw with Nathan, are an
effective and crushing means of exercising moral power. Christ
understood that men do not modify their personal points of
view toward a social point of view by benevolence alone; power moves them.

Moral power may be used to move men from their personal
viewpoints to a social viewpoint because it is a means of in-
vesting them with tolerance and a commitment to justice. This
is not surprising, for moral power, we learned, is the power of
infusing in Jack Micro an understanding of someone else's
point of view, and, at its ultimate, of stilling the influence, at
least temporarily, of Micro's own point of view.

I want now to trace more exactly the relation between understanding and the tandem virtues, justice and tolerance.

Justice is the cool side of tolerance or, put in another way,
tolerance is the warm side of justice. It is one thing to recognize that other persons have interests which merit fulfillment;

it is another thing to feel strongly about it. Some men passionately seek justice for others; they join revolutionary parties, or
demonstrate, or commit civil disobedience and go to jail because of it. Tolerance makes the heart grow fonder of justice.

Understanding, we saw, has two aspects, the aspect of
knowing and the aspect of feeling. When we fully and warmly
understand a person, we not only know his facts, interests, and
moral-relatents, we also experience the feelings which transform his beliefs into convictions, his interests into passions,
and his moral-relatents into commitments. These two aspects
of understanding run in the same traces in which the tandem
virtues run. Tolerance is to the feeling aspect of understanding as justice is to its knowing aspect. Fully infusing another's
point of view into a person means that he becomes so palpably
and nearly identical with that person that he wishes everything for that person that the person wishes for himself, and
nothing can so fire the furnace of tolerance nor so clarify the
lens of justice as this identification through understanding.
Small wonder, then, that I have claimed moral power to be
the chief instrument in attaining a just and tolerant society.
Those cities that exercise moral power for good are in light;
they bask in tolerance and justice; the others live in darkness,
untolerated and undefended. Those who live in darkness
drop from sight.

Imagine only half the people being brought to an understanding of the other half! Imagine only half the people being
brought to a state of tolerance and desire for justice for the
other half!

Unequal access to moral power makes some of us masters
and of others it makes slaves, or indulged pets.

Our city will not have a dynamic sense of community unless
each member in it has access to moral power. Without that
power an inhabitant has no ability to peacefully turn his city
toward justice and tolerance; without that power, he is a helpless victim, and that gives him neither a sense of dynamism

nor a sense of community. If understanding is the relation which unifies neighborhoods into a city, and if every inhabitant has the right to play a role and to be understood, then each person must have the power to tie himself to others *via* understanding.

In the next chapter, I will examine what contribution art, and, in the last chapter, what contribution philosophy can make to creating social understanding among neighborhoods and, thereby, unifying cities. Since social understanding is a relation established in thought, it is not surprising that art and philosophy should and can play key roles. Their civic role admittedly has been slight in our cities; however, this is due not as much to their ineffectiveness as to the fact that most persons' conception of a city's function has excluded their use. In my conception of a city, their role is necessary and effective because they provide access to moral power. A city, in my conception, is not a legal federation of neighborhoods; rather, a city's neighborhoods are federated in the understanding.

I am suggesting that we lay aside the legalistic contract theory of cities that has dominated our thought—and which has excluded the contributions of art and philosophy—and move to an understanding theory of unity. The latter, but not the contract theory, lures a person outside his own being into a warm social understanding wherein he can sense his community. I will show, now, how art and philosophy can help create social understanding.

14 THE DETRIVIALIZATION OF THE ARTS

Ther is mor tew arte than metes the eye, ear, nowes, or tonge.
—FANEBIUS PERLYNG

If we lean on the genius of the arts while trying to unify the Many neighborhoods into One city, we can detrivialize the arts. Most people, unfortunately, now believe that the arts are trivial and ineffective. Art has been reduced to this undeserved low estate by a theory I call aestheticism. Aestheticism has expropriated the word "art": It takes "art" to be synonymous with "fine art"; it refuses to call anything "art" which does not have positive aesthetic value. I wrest control of the word "art" from aestheticism and restore it to a more potent use. That use reflects my belief that the arts are uniquely suited to generating understanding by exercising moral power, which, if used to infuse points of view, may once again play a moral, social, and political role in the city.

❦ ❦ ❦

To FULLY APPRECIATE how trivial the arts are now thought to be, imagine all the world's paintings and sculptures, and their reproductions, destroyed; imagine the world's musical scores burned, all records and tapes melted, and memory of compositions wholly obliterated; imagine the total erasure of memory and notation of all except folk dances; imagine all the novels and plays consumed, and poems as well; and imagine all film reduced to static dust. The mass of the world's art would be no more absent from most Americans' lives than it is now when our museums, libraries, and performing houses are filled with the sight, sound, and body of the arts. True piety and reverence for the traces of past civilizations is shared by few, and most look on the arts as mere decoration, a toy of the idle, the bauble of the rich, relief for the bored, trips for foolish antiquarians, and jobs for a few teachers of literature and the arts.

The prestige arts in our society address such a small percentage of the people who are so vapidly served by narcissistic artists that anyone who suggests that the chief value of the arts is moral and social is likely to be met with a stare usually reserved for Communists or Puritans. We have poets reading to each other; painters strung out by gallery agents carefully guarding lists of $50,000 (and up) income-per-year patrons; playwrights knowingly eying the tastes of out-of-town, New York Broadway expense-account audiences; Sol Hurok prodigies skimming the cream by mastering melodies principally composed in earlier centuries; and sylphs and muscles silver-slippering and rump-rubbing their way around stages set for plucked highbrows.

With the arts in such a state, it seems frivolous and absurd to suggest that the arts might make a significant contribution to the unification of our cities. It is usually assumed that people would rather polish their cars, open a can of beer and watch television, fiddle with their tall short-wave sets, drink at the local bar, play cards or re-read the evening news, smoke MaryJohn and stare, or goggle through *Playboy*.

The arts will not be rescued from triviality, nor artists escape being made moral and political eunuchs, unless the dominant theory of art held by journalists, critics, academic overlords, and fine art panderers is retired. That theory is what I shall call "aestheticism."

Aestheticism is bad, but not all bad. To show that art was not trivialized by evil intent, I want to show how in their attempt to defend artistic freedom honorable men were dialectically seduced into aestheticism.

Every American who reads newspapers and magazines has read how countries with a Communist government hold art in thrall. They have been told that Communist doctrine demands that art serve one and only one purpose, namely, to present the social and political views currently held by the government.

We have also read that there has been an artistic "thaw" in many Communist countries. This thaw has been a response to demands that the arts and artists be freed. We who live in a democracy look on these demands for freedom with sympathy; we tend to see our artistic freedom as evidence of the superiority of our society over Communist society.

Yet, in considering the Puritan attitude toward art, we notice that even in anti-Communist democracies many people share something of the Communist view. Artists, according to the Puritan view, should not have unlimited freedom. Artists should not produce or at least should not be allowed to distribute anything which offends conventional morality or taste. Censorship trials, demands for the removal of sculpture from museums, the sequestering of some books in locked "special collection" rooms of libraries, oak leaf clusters on brave male genitalia, age limits on movie patrons, and harassment of theatre companies who show sacred persons—such as the Pope or Winston Churchill—in a critical light, demonstrate that even in "free societies" people limit artists' freedom when its exercise comes into conflict with their moral, social, and political views.

Clearly enough, the Communist-Puritan strictures on art and artists would be quite irrelevant if art could not in fact purvey moral, social, and political matter. Artists' viewpoints may be lodged in works of art. Their being there and being what they are is what makes them objectionable to the Communist-Puritan.

On what grounds can a defender of artistic freedom stand if he would ward off the attacks of Communists, Puritans, and Fascists? Particularly if he is not willing to defend what is immoral, politically revolutionary, or socially pernicious. His chief recourse is to deny that the only or main value of the arts derives from their moral, social, and political utility. He has to find their chief value in a different aspect of the arts, and maintain that art's premier value is its aesthetic value. The familiar phrase, "Art for art's sake," expresses succinctly the belief that aesthetic value is the primary value of art.

The aesthetic value of objects is associated primarily with the gratification they supply our senses. It is a value familiar to all of us. Most Americans can appreciate the strong grace some football halfbacks have when they run; millions of our countrymen head for the mountains and their lakes and streams because they enjoy the sight and sound of these natural beauties; the visual attractiveness of automobiles offers another example of aesthetic value to which a large number of Americans are sensitive, auto sales rising and falling on the acceptability of new designs.

Of course, we recognize that objects may simultaneously have more than one kind of value; they may have moral, intellectual, economic, and practical values as well as aesthetic value; and, moreover, these different kinds of value may be independent of one another. An object may be high in one or more of the values and low in others. For example, that graceful halfback may, at the same time, be one of the cruelest and most intelligent of men; to the mad lumber baron, those beautiful redwoods may be less interesting for their aesthetic value than they are for their timber; and that sleek automobile may turn out to be a mechanical headache to its despairing owner.

By claiming that the aesthetic value of artistic works overrides their moral and political offensiveness to government officials and Puritans, the defender of artistic freedom may claim that plays, movies, dances, poems, or novels should be exempt from moral and political restraints. The real test of the aesthete's tolerance comes when he is asked to help suppress art which is immoral and devoid of aesthetic value. The ugly often dampens his freedom fires unless he is willing to take up new dialectical ground on the hillock of taste.

If aesthetic value is a matter of taste, then, it can be argued, since taste varies, what may be ugly to our freedom fighter may be beautiful to another. Unless he provides an objective way of deciding on the correctness of taste judgments, the aesthete should be willing to defend anyone who produces anything which is beautiful to someone's taste. The limits of artistic freedom have to be as wide as the taste for the beautiful.

The dialectical defense of artistic freedom has carried us to the edge of taste. This, however, may be too great a distance to travel. Compared with other kinds of value, the values appealing to taste are rather trivial. In a contest of values, where two kinds of value must compete with each other—both being desired, but only one of them actually attainable—aesthetic value is usually the lesser value. For example, though we all like handsome cars, being able to afford only one, we realize that the designers' work must give pride of place to the engineers'; one-car owners do not want to own an unsafe bucket of loose bolts no matter how handsome it is. And we would think an automobile manufacturer who placed aesthetic over safety value as morally culpable. Moreover, we would punish him by not buying his cars again.

Considering how relatively trivial aesthetic value is, the effect of making the value of taste uppermost is to trivialize art. Whatever other functions art may have, and, historically, they have been many—to instruct, entertain, reveal profound truths, influence, morally improve, communicate, sell, inspire, purify the soul, relieve tensions, sharpen our sense discrimination, bring humans heart to heart—these functions, when demoted to a status below aesthetic titillation, are trivialized. And so art is trivialized.

Our retracing of the dialectical seduction of art appreciators and aestheticians has revealed honorable intentions: Democratic artistic freedom must be defended, and it can be defended against the forces of crabbed suppression if the aesthetic value of art objects is made their chief value. The dialectic doesn't end here, however, for aestheticians and philosophers of art don't want to trivialize the arts in the process of defending them. Many are aware that surrendering art exclusively to the tyranny of taste for mere beauty of appearance trivializes the arts. Their desire to prevent trivialization accounts in part for the widespread advocacy and acceptance of an expression theory of art.

The expression theory of art views an artist's productions as expressions, primarily, of the artist's and/or society's feelings and emotions. Emotions and feelings are stressed over ideas, because if the theory is to apply to all the arts, it must surely apply to instrumental music and abstract painting, and it is difficult to maintain that they express theories or moral reflections. In addition, the arts are thought to backstop and supplement language which many consider weakest in the expression, or, at least, the description, of feeling and emotion.

The term "express" has its primary application to language. We say that sentences express what we mean; we say we use language to express ourselves. Few would doubt the high value of language in the human enterprise; thus, if art objects are similar to language in sharing an expressive, and, presumably, communicative, function, then the arts too must have a high value.

An expression theory of art is supposed to detrivialize art. The arguments go like this:

Expressive value is not trivial.
Expressive value and aesthetic value are identical.
Therefore, aesthetic value is not trivial.

If aesthetic value is not trivial, art is not trivial.
Aesthetic value, we have just proved, is not trivial.
Therefore art is not trivial.

The most vulnerable premiss is the second premiss of the first argument. The stature of art appears to depend on it. Are expressive and aesthetic value one and the same? They do not seem to be. Curses are expressive, indeed, often painfully so, but they may also be ugly as sin. And sunsets are beautiful, yet of whom are they expressive? That Great Artist up yonder? Not many would wish a return to Sunday School theology in order to defend the identity of expressive and aesthetic value.

If expressive and aesthetic value are not one and the same, but distinct and independent, we are faced with a dilemma: Either aesthetic value is primary or expressive value is primary. If aesthetic value is primary, then the expression theory of art has failed to detrivialize art. This puts us right back where we were. If expressive value is primary, and distinct from aesthetic value, then the expression theory is not a theory of the aesthetic value of art objects. But, if it is not a theory of aesthetic value, how can it be a theory of the *art* in art objects? Mustn't a purported theory of art do justice to aesthetic artistry if it is to be a theory of art?

In short, if expressive value is primary, an expression theory of art paradoxically ignores the "art" in "art object."

Put baldly, here's our dilemma: Emphasis on the aesthetic value of art objects trivializes them; emphasis on any other value, such as expressiveness, while detrivializing them, severs them from their artistry.

Put still more baldly: Art is either trivial or, if not trivial, it isn't art. Aestheticism, here is thy sting!

Surely, there must be a way out of such a ridiculous impasse.

Surely, art need not be trivial, and, surely, something's being art shouldn't make it trivial. Is there another dialectical route besides the one which led to aestheticism?

I think there is another such route. And the first step on it toward the detrivialization of art is this: We must refuse to answer "Indeed" to the following insidious question, "What is the point of calling anything a work of art if it is not to indicate an object with aesthetic merit?" Don't answer "Indeed"!

The citizenry has lost the power of art because it has capitulated to the aesthetes. Our citizenry has given the aesthetes full and exclusive patent on the word "art." And this is the rule aesthetes have laid down for the use of the word "art":

> *If and only if an object has aesthetic value is it to be called art.*

I shall call this the Aesthete Rule. It lies at the center of aestheticism.

Those of us who wish to rescue art from the triviality which aestheticism has visited on it must replace the Aesthete Rule with a different rule. We must re-possess the word "art," and we must learn to break a habit governed by the Aesthete Rule: When people talk about paintings, or sculpture, or music, or novels, or movies, we must not assume that they are talking about aesthetically good objects.

When critics, writing under the influence of the Aesthete Rule, say that a play is bad, don't conclude that it is not art. The absence of aesthetic value does not condemn a play to the status of a non-art object.

When critics, writing under the influence of the Aesthete Rule, say that a painting is good, don't conclude that "good" means only "aesthetically good." Until further specification, let "good" have all the rich ambiguity it deserves. Things can be good in many ways.

Stop equating art with fine art. And stop equating fine art

with art objects praised by top-of-the-pecking-order critics for their aesthetic value.

Stiffen your spine by remembering how appropriate you think it is to say that a play is "moving," that a movie is "searing," that a poem is "profound," that music has "soul," that an opera is "eloquent," that a dance is an "exploration of tragic *angst*," that a novel is "comic," or that a painting is "symbolic." These are human terms, not narrowly aesthetic terms. When such human terms are applicable to an object, it is legitimate to say of that object that it is an "art" object; "beautiful" isn't the only term with the power to transmute "object" into "art object."

Objects which are "moving," "searing," "profound," "soul" possessing, "eloquent," "symbolic," "comic," or an "exploration of tragic *angst*" are not trivial. If it is in virtue of the applicability of such human terms that objects are to be considered "art" objects, and, so, art, then art is not trivial.

My feelings are at high tide here because I am trying to break the hold which the Aesthete Rule has had on me. I have too long unthinkingly thought of art almost solely in terms of things which have high aesthetic merit, as if that were the sole criterion for calling anything art. My thinking has been imprisoned by a Rule which has sentenced me to a cell of which Mister Acceptable Taste is the warden. I have lived in jail under the illusion that I have been free. And so have others.

Many of us have been caught in the net of "Great Art." And swimming about in the public aquarium as captive, tastevaine species, we tend to pity the crude fare to which the multitude of unnetted fish still at sea are condemned. While the netted fatten on Great Art supplied by art entrepreneurs, the unnetted subsist on more popular fare. After all, whom should the artists serve, the netted or the unnetted? Fame and immortality are the spurs; fatten the aquarium trumpet fishes and they will oblige by capitalizing and piping your ART into a GREAT future. As for the unnetted, roaming free and un-sold in the sea, let them eat commercial.

Encouragingly, there are artists who feel an obligation to the unnetted as much as or more than to the netted. In their struggle to break the Aesthete Rule, they often try to justify their attempt at revolt by exaggerating the capabilities of the unnetted: "Great Art speaks to *all* people of all ages." Thus are we subtly shown the deep-down domestication of the artist who would be free of the tyranny of taste, still bowing and scraping to Great Art.

Realistically, we cannot expect the unnetted to apotheosize Great Art because it is alien to them. Great Art is, in the main, art preserved from the past by persons schooled in the arts and history of art, and perhaps the period in which the art was created. To feel familiar with much Great Art requires a knowledge gained by fairly extensive training or a lot of lei-sure spent listening, seeing, and talking. The unnetted gen-erally, and understandably, have not acquired this historical knowledge and, so, do not appreciate many of these monu-ments of the past. We should not be surprised that for the unnetted the prestige arts are in the main trivial.

Further, I cannot see much upcoming change in the Great-Art-readiness of the unnetted. The arts and their history are frozen out of the school curriculum except for those few stu-dents who display talent or are pushed or given private les-sons by their parents. Post-Sputnik curricula still pull a tight noose on the arts. The sparse contact which students have with literature and the arts in public school becomes even thinner once they leave school, for the arts have no natural function to play in the lives of most American people except as entertainment; and entertainment is only one of the many and lesser functions which art might perform. In fact, enter-tainment value may have a lower ranking than aesthetic value.

But there is no obstacle to prevent the unnetted from mak-

ing sophisticated judgments about art provided that it is relevant to their lives; for, in that event, they have a knowledge
which they can bring to bear upon art. The unnetted are mistakenly thought incapable of appreciating art because they
are not prepared to "Ah" at Great Art.

There is no great barrier to grasping the art of, for example,
a play or a novel. A play pitched to our lives, something of
which we have knowledge, is pitching to our strong side. That
knowledge has been acquired without formal education, and
if pitched to, does bring forth a sophisticated judgment and
appreciation; the art of the play enhances rather than detracts
from what the author and players present.

The greatest deterrent to the production of good art for the
unnetted is not their "ignorance," untutored "taste," or indifference; it is artists' ignorance of and indifference toward the
life-knowledge of the unnetted. Artists should produce in accord with the Life Rule and on the portal entrance to the new
world of art they must place a warning to devotees of aestheticism: Abandon the Aesthete Rule, all ye who enter here.

The form of the arts, for example, drama, music or sculpture—that which distinguishes one art form from another—
is not a barrier surmountable only by the netted. The form of
the drama is what makes a play a play and not another thing,
and that is no great mystery. Mastering a form enough to
write and produce a good play is difficult, but it is not the art
of the form that deters the audience from appreciation. What
does deter appreciation is irrelevant, obscure, or esoteric substance clinging to the frame of the arts. A black, contemporary
audience, not given to fantasies, isn't exactly turned on by
the problems encountered by a titled family facing the prospect of their son and heir marrying a commoner; it isn't the
art of the drama which turns them away from the play. What
does excite appreciation and sophisticated judgment is Doug-
las Turner Ward's *Happy Ending*, a portrayal of the disaster
which hits a circle of people depending on the income and

side benefits of a woman in domestic service about to lose her job with a rich couple because the husband is going to break up their marriage, having caught his wife in bed with her paramour. And that's a play.

The word "art," instead of being narrowly circumscribed by the Aesthete Rule, must be allowed a use as wide as that which we allow to the phrase "art form." Drama is one art form; music another; painting still another, and so forth. A bad play is still art, for a play is an instance of an art form.

We recognize that art objects have possibly multiple functions—to instruct, entertain, express, and so forth. Do not pick out one function, for example, the expressive, and make it a Rule on the pattern of the Aesthete Rule in order to once again narrow the use of "art." An unentertaining play is still art, for a play is an instance of an art form. Keep the use of "art" wide enough to accommodate the fact that an art form lends itself to many functions. The breadth of and humanness of the words we use to praise or condemn art products—searing, profound, eloquent, comic, moving, symbolic—shows us how untrivial art, if broadly enough conceived, is and can be.

Finding that "art," when as broadly conceived as "art form," is no deterrent to sophisticated appreciation, we recognize that the detrivialization of art depends upon the willingness of artists to learn about and address themselves to the life-knowledge of the unnetted and netted.

What are the unnetted? Persons. And what do we call that which makes the perils of domestic service more important to some people than the troubles of a titled-commoner marriage? A point of view. Art, if broadly conceived, may serve every point of view, and every aspect of a point of view, including the factual aspect, the interest aspect with its attendant immanent emotions, and the moral aspect with its attendant transcendent emotions. Art should be as pertinent as a newspaper.

Home at last. Art is detrivialized if artists arm it with the moral power of which it is capable. Art becomes important when it becomes dangerous; it becomes dangerous when it has the power to change a city.

Art is capable of moral power because it is particularly suited to infusing a point of view into its audience. When this happens, the unifying relation of understanding between neighborhoods is created. Art, therefore, can be a powerful instrument in transforming the Many neighborhoods into One city. Cities of the world, art is not your luxury that you may wear as an adornment to seduce the people of the world to be your tourists; art is a practical necessity which you must use if you are to turn your inhabitants into citizens and if you are to transcend the emotions that presently divide us.

Having broken the ideological hold of the Aesthete Rule over art, artists, and ourselves, free now to conjure with art in broader terms, we can think of art exercising moral power without pitting it against misconceived aesthetic restraints; cleansed of the dilemma inherited from the expressive theory, we can seriously advocate the proposition that the arts can make a significant contribution to the creation of a unified city. I want now to explain specifically, but briefly, why the arts are a political weapon.

The arts can play a political, moral, and social role because of their unique effectiveness in infusing a point of view into persons. First, they are peculiarly able to present a point of view in all its thickness and warmth, delivering a point of view with its emotions, immanent and transcendent, almost wholly intact. Secondly, because art gives public, sensuous embodiment to a private point of view with its wraithlike, elusive emotional vapors, it serves as a supplement to our own imagination, often too weak to justly summon another's point of view before our mind. And thirdly, art presents a point of view at a distance; a point of view is staged for us and we can contemplate it operating before us without being drawn into the action on stage as we would be in real life; for a moment, we can indulge the luxury of contemplation without feeling the immediate pressure to act.

With regard to my first point, the arts form a hierarchy, their ranking based on an art form's ability to present all the aspects of a point of view. The more complex art forms have all the advantage here. The cinema and opera incorporate several of the arts—drama, music, and visual power. Instrumental music and abstract art have to take lowest rank in their ability to present all the aspects of a point of view, presenting almost solely the immanent feelings and emotions. They are the most aesthetic of the arts, and in themselves possess the least moral power. They may become a symbolic badge because of what we know about their origin and acceptability among a group of persons, as, for example, soul music is the badge of a certain group of Black people in the United States.

The art forms using language have to rank near the top of the hierarchy because they can present the factual and moral aspects of a point of view as nothing else can. The vines of language lash a point of view into an assemblage in which men minded to do so may discover themselves.

The novel, poetry, drama are not reports from a laboratory; they are thick with feeling and emotion. When art presents emotions and feelings, they are forced out of our inward closets and into outward physical embodiment—this grimace on the actor's face, a harsh groan, the gutty scrape of the cello, a trembling diaphram projected by the sheen of a taut leotard.

Once afloat in the luminous space of art, these emotions are no longer blindly immanent, but lifted to a transcendent level, captured, and dominated in an art form designed by a mind insatiable for mind-digested nature. Whereas the body takes in food and excretes waste, the mind ingests nature and delivers the crystal of art, that crystal wherein nature is ordered by and for thought.

The emotions and feelings captured by art may be portrayed as immanent for the persons suffering or enjoying them, but we, the audience and spectators, know them to be outside us; and because the artist has created a sensuous, exterior counterpart for the emotions, and has placed and manipulated them for his own purposes, they have become artificial, controlled, and, thereby, transcendent. Those immanent emotions become corrected and transformed for us; their corrected transformation makes them fit to be moral emotions and feelings. Immanent rage turns to transcendent outrage; passion becomes love; jealousy changes to guarded trust; frustration is laughed into humor; fear flakes into the excitement of adventure. Cities, deliver our emotional vapors into the hands of artists who care for us, for all of us. " 'Consider, dear sir,' cries Jones, in a trembling voice." Neglect us no more to the rude hands of advertising, propaganda, soap operas, and advertisers' television.

My second reason for freighting the arts with such a heavy civic burden rests on the fact that nothing else produced by humans serves so well to supplement our imagination of what it is to be another person. My daughter, Megan, chin on the back of our couch, musing about *Crime and Punishment*: "You feel about Dostoyevsky's people as you do about real people. You suffer with them, feel their agony and sorrow." Bridging our massive ignorance and enlarging our meager imagination, the artist can make those who are normally alien to our experience come to life for us. And once they have lodged in our understanding, they press against its narrow walls, insisting on a place until our memory fades or our heart hardens.

The stretch which the arts can give to our imagination shouldn't be underestimated. What is it like to have a fish's point of view, or a bird's, or perhaps an ant's? Or even a badger's? For those interested, I suggest reading the first book of *The Once and Future King*, ("The Sword in the Stone," chapters 5, 8, 13, 18, and 21) T. H. White's version of the King Arthur legend. Part of King Arthur's education, overseen by

Merlyn, is to learn to understand everything over which he will have dominion. It is for this reason that Merlyn turns Wart, the young King Arthur, into a perch, a merlin, then an owl and a wild goose, into an ant, and a badger. You can read about these animals' point of view so imaginatively projected by White that you can believe you can get yourself a surrogate education about them.

Certain human events that have occurred and are likely to re-occur must be understood. Some men and women and children will rebel, revolt, riot, pillage, burn, loot, curse, hit, be arrested, beaten, killed, wounded, alienated further, will return to their former condition, and hate more than ever. Why do they do these things and why do such reprisals occur?

We have got to understand. We have got to get inside their point of view and feel it as passionately as we can. It is absolutely necessary that artists put themselves to the job of presenting that point of view. We must know the facts lodged in that point of view, the needs, desires, and interests webbed within it and the strength of the attendant immanent emotions measured in terms of their heat. And we must know the moral-relatents which give their acts the spine of justice and honor. We have got to face the inevitability of what the close-up shows us: A cursing, tear-spattered man reaching for an avenging equalizer.

My third point about art's distance dovetails here. A movie which presents us the point of view of a modern American revolutionary does not require our simultaneous involvement. We do not need to adopt at that moment the defenses which a face-to-face encounter would evoke. Our own point of view can be laid aside during the showing, inoperative, while the presented point of view has its way with us and enables us to live momentarily within another viewpoint. The distance of art does what the parable does; it anesthetizes our own point of view, changes it from being the substance of our own subjectivity into an object that we judge from the new point of view. Instead of having the subjectivity of ownership, our point of view has the objectivity of otherness. It came as a surprise to David to be told that "Thou art the man." It comes as a surprise to many of us that we are that "honkey."

In summary, I have shown how for most people art is trivial and explained why this triviality has made it difficult to believe that art may play an important moral and political role in our city. Then I retraced the dialectical trail to aestheticism trod by men desirous to defend artistic freedom. After finding that an expression theory cannot detrivialize art if art remains governed by the Aesthete Rule, I pleaded for a broader conception of the art and artists' responsibility so that the arts might be detrivialized. Finally, I specified the special features of art which makes it peculiarly suitable for generating understanding and exercising moral power.

15 THE FIRES OF PHILOSOPHY

Tyger! Tyger! Burne thee bryght!
—FANEBIUS PERLYNG

My thesis in this concluding chapter is that philosophizing is the highest civic virtue we can practice. Philosophy is the verbal process of concinnating conflicting personal points of view into a consistent social point of view. Its function is the unification of society, a function which cannot be performed by the few for the many, but requires the participation of the many. Only the Many can make themselves One through reason.

※ ※ ※

A SHARP SHIFT in the attitude toward philosophy occurred when Plato took the toga from Socrates. That shift marks the division between the "Socratic" dialogues of Plato and the "Platonic" dialogues of Plato. For Socrates and his friends, it appears that philosophy was distilled when they discoursed critically, carefully, and wittily with each other. Philosophy emerged as high level discourse on subjects that citizens thought important. For Plato, on the other hand, philosophy became a subject matter. It was something for which one was trained; it was thought difficult and capable of attainment only by an elite few. Plato moved philosophy out of the agora, the market place, and into the academy.

Plato's attitude toward philosophy was pictured most vividly in his own Allegory of the Cave. He likened the philosophically ignorant to persons chained in a cave. Behind them sculpted likenesses of objects were carried to and fro, the shadows of the likenesses being cast on the wall in front of the chained persons. The prisoners, being unable to turn their heads, had to form their ideas of reality from the likenesses' shadows alone. Compare the prisoners' knowledge to that of a person who had been released from the cave and had walked about in the sunlit world observing and inspecting the objects themselves. Surely his knowledge of reality would be superior to that of the prisoners! For Plato, the philosopher is like the man who was taken from the cave and the unphilosophical are those who remained prisoners.

For Plato, only by long training may man escape the cave of opinion and achieve philosophical knowledge. Given the notion that few attain philosophical knowledge and given the notion that that kind of knowledge is superior, it is an easy step to Plato's view that, in the ideal state, governance should be handed to those who really know, that is, to the philosopher-kings.

It is evident that in our own day philosophy has followed Plato's course rather than Socrates'. Philosophy is an academic subject matter; it is listed in college and university catalogues. People are tested for their knowledge of philosophical subject matter as well as their philosophical skill. Philosophy has been professionalized.

The shift from Socrates to Plato also changed philosophy from a spoken to a written practice. The transition was misleadingly subtle, for in deference to Socrates' verbal hegemony, Plato wrote in dialogue style, but write he did. The literary effort to make the dialogue style seem natural presses the writer closer to oral intelligibility than a monologue style does.

Naturalness is most easily achieved if the dialogue can ascend from a common incident, a chance remark, or an innocent encounter; this makes the written matter more pertinent and available to the non-professional reader than a scholastic style does. Compare the intelligibility for non-professionals of Platonic dialogue *versus* Aristotelian monologue.

Writing, even in dialogue style, however, may be at best a springboard for philosophizing; it can never be its leap. Emphasis on written "philosophy" breeds undue emphasis on doctrine. If a piece of philosophical writing is not a springboard or a report of some remarkable philosophical conversation, its only reason for being is to set down and argue for doctrine. The most I will concede is that the typical philosophical tract is a pseudo-dialogue; in it the writer usually addresses and argues against other persons' doctrines and conclusions which he believes are inconsistent with his own. Thus, through doctrinaire, pseudo-dialogue does philosophy become subject matter; students must read, learn, paraphrase, memorize, recite, explicate, analyze, refute, and assess the doctrines and arguments of eminent philosophers. He who has never been a student of philosophy is frozen out of this philosophical activity because he has not the background "knowledge" which enables him to be a certified participant. Philosophy scandalously retires to the thin ranks of the academic professionals when it freezes extemporaneous speech into studied doctrines.

Under the Platonic conception of philosophy, the continued existence of philosophy is guaranteed by the continuity of the teacher-student relationship. The teacher, master of doctrines past and present, passes on his philosophical knowledge and skill to his student, who in turn becomes teacher to the next generation. For the Platonist, the disappearance of the schools would knell the end of philosophy.

That the Platonic conception of philosophy has not usurped the whole of philosophy is evident enough to anyone who recalls that non-professional philosophers still ask about the meaning of life, wonder about the beginning of the universe and the existence of god, worry about whether or not they are mere machines, stew about the nature of the good life, debate about abortion, contraceptives, and capital punishment, and read Nietzsche, Ortega y Gasset, Hesse, Sartre, Marcuse, Walter Lippman, Ayn Rand, R. D. Laing, Kierkegaard, and Coleridge. Young men and women sensing their growing intellectual powers, middle aged men and women scanning the burnt butts of their youthful ambitions, and old men and women facing nothingness have always staffed a philosophic, Socratic underground.

My own sympathies are with the Socratic underground but my respect goes to the professionals. Against the Platonic conception, I do not think philosophy should be the exclusive possession of an élite, it should not be professionalized, it should live primarily in verbal discourse rather than written prose, it should not be confined to the academy, it should not consist of doctrines, and its continued existence should not depend upon historical mothballing. Against the Socratic underground I think that philosophy should be better than that which the underground produces.

Plato's Allegory of the Cave is a powerful image. It has given imaginative sanctions to an élitist view of philosophy and philosophers. Whoever wishes to break the Platonist hold on philosophy would be well advised to invent a counter-allegory which sanctions the more democratic, Socratic underground conception of philosophy.

Such a counter-allegory would have to include elements which would dignify the mass of amateurs *versus* the élite professionals, back the agora *versus* the academy, advertise the verbal *versus* the written, support current relevance *versus* historical reverence, and celebrate concinnity *versus* doctrine.

❋   ❋   ❋

THE ALLEGORY OF THE FIRE

Imagine a cave in which men are prisoners, able to see only the shadows of likenesses of objects. They had heard once of a man who had been set free, or, as some said, who had broken free. It was told of him that he had claimed to have found that it was a "cave" in which they lived as "prisoners," that he knew this because he had found an "exit" from the cave, and that in leaving the cave by the exit he had found a "world" outside the cave, and that in the world there was what he called a "knowledge sun."

Upon being asked why he called it a "knowledge sun," the escapee answered that he called it that because once he saw the world by the light of the sun, he realized that while in the cave all he had ever seen were shadows of likenesses of original objects, and that only by observing these originals in the light of the sun could one have any knowledge of their nature.

Some wanted to know, especially the metaphysicians, on what basis he claimed there existed these three things, "shadows," "likenesses of objects," and "original objects." He said that in the light of the knowledge sun he had seen the originals, he had seen the likenesses, and he had seen their shadows; and, further, he had seen them simultaneously.

Among these prisoners, as among any group of men, there were skeptics. Why, they asked, should anyone take the claims of a "hearsay" escapee seriously? All his purported talk of "colors," "three dimensions," and "weight" was nonsense, meaningless; no one had ever experienced any of these things, and, consequently, could have no idea at all of what the words stood for. After all, said the skeptics, we have light in our world and we see all there is to see. Furthermore, they inquired, what evidence do we have for believing there is an exit from "the cave" and another world outside except the word of a supposed escapee?

Here the discussion was taken up by the revolutionaries who warned the prisoners to beware of believing a man who claimed to have escaped from his chains but who did not free anyone else. Surely, they cried, here is a man not to be trusted; here is a man who wishes to rule the others and knows it will be easier to do so if he can convince the prisoners that he has special knowledge to which they are not privy. A moral man would release the prisoners, lead them to the exit, out into the world, and let them share the knowledge revealed by that marvelous "sun."

The metaphysicians among the prisoners speculated boldly; perhaps, they said, there are likenesses and originals in what the escapee had called their cave. Perhaps, said the most speculative, the cave is the world.

But one could never verify this, scoffed the skeptics.

We could verify this, said the scientists, if we increased the fire light and made it as bright as the "knowledge sun." Then we would be able to see as well as the escapee claimed to have seen.

Some prisoners urged the others to stop dwelling upon these stories from another time and to find out the truth of the matter for themselves. They advocated a cooperative effort of the prisoners to free themselves. Once one man was free, he should, as the revolutionaries proclaimed, help others to be free, and they in turn should free all the rest. Then they would search for the exit.

The prisoners took heart at this, and in their newly won confidence succeeded in setting each other free. With soaring spirits they set off in all directions, seeking for an exit. Rumors of exits circulated, only to be found baseless again and again. After all the previous discussion, no one was rash enough to claim personally that he had found an exit and had gone out into the world and was now returned to tell them about it. The peoples' paths crossed and recrossed and none could or would say he had found an exit.

They lost heart for the search and men began to say more and more frequently that perhaps the cave is the world as the metaphysicians said. That would explain why they had not found an exit, for there is no exit from the world. And it seemed to follow that if there is no world outside the world, there is no knowledge sun either. And without a knowledge sun, there can be no way of knowing whether likenesses and objects exist, said the skeptics.

The world is a dark, shadowy cave, said the skeptics. It has no exit, said the realists. We are doomed, whined the Cassandras. If only we had more light, wished the scientists. The same group of prisoners who earlier had urged cooperation to free themselves from their chains now urged a new cooperative effort. They went among the other prisoners, talking with them patiently, reasoning calmly, suggesting that by a common effort they could make more light and, thereby, gain more knowledge about their cave-world. Men, they said, must mend their present divisions and form a community. This random wandering in the shadowy cave and the casual relations with each other that netted only wishful rumors about found exits or glum complaints about their dark doom could be ended if they would form a true community. With a true community, they could gain useful knowledge.

Because these patient, reasonable men held knowledge in such high regard, and because they made it so tantalizing to the other cave dwellers, they were dubbed philosophers, a name coming from the language of one group of cave dwellers; for them "philos" meant "love" and "sophia" meant "wisdom."

Out of the philosophers' talk came a community of talkers and out of their talk came moral community, and out of moral community came communal action. As our helicopter lifts off the pad, we see below a great, bright fire which they call the "illumination." People are ringed around the illumination, each throwing a faggot on the fire; others are converging on the fire, everyone carrying faggots; still others are fetching faggots. And the cave is bright and the people are cheerful and free. Above the popping exhaust of our helicopter engine, we hear this chant, "Color, community, and the third dimension. Color, community, and the third dimension. Color, community, and . . ."

* * *

The supreme end of philosophizing is the creation of community. That is a civic end requiring the participation of all; community cannot be created by a few professional philosophers, for one man can no more concinnate for another than he can love for him.

The philosophic crisis we face is a crisis of choice. The time will be on us when we cannot avoid choosing between work and concinnation. This is a social choice, not merely an individual one. If this choice is to be based on transcendent reasons rather than immanent emotions, we cannot make it until we have publicly reasoned about the two forms of life and about the kind of society that will make it possible to lead the kind of life we finally choose. Failure to participate in this philosophizing means that you have left your choice of life and society for others to make. Everyone has a faggot for the fire.

Since not everyone is in the academy, the widespread philosophizing I advocate can never occur until philosophizing occurs as naturally in the city as it does in the academy. After all, better to be hung in the market place or neighborhood for philosophizing there than to expire of safe age in the sanctuary of the academy.

The dream of universal philosophizing will remain meager fantasy unless philosophy becomes vital to our social agonies. Philosophy's vitality can be restored only by the same kind of forces that originally brought it into existence. (Philosophy did not always exist.) Philosophy was originally squeezed into existence by the jaws of controversy mashing down on matters of importance to persons living in a society which prided itself on reasoning and which was forced into reasoning its way to community. Cities of free men in Greece were struggling to slip out of their rural cocoon and into a new phase of existence as centers of trade and commerce. In the ensuing struggle for power and advantage, when naked, physical power was insufficient, factions were forced to talk and argue. When the talk and argument became sophisticated enough, philosophy emerged.

I will illustrate this thesis about the origin of philosophy by reconstructing a political controversy which occurred in ancient Athens. I shall try to show how the jaws of controversy squeezed some metaphysics and theory of knowledge out of Plato. This reconstruction is based on an interpretation of some of Plato's *The Republic.*

Think for a moment of Plato's epistemological and metaphysical flirtation with the Ideas—those remote, objective, abstract, perfect concepts—as his ultimate, most sophisticated and imaginative defense of the nobility's point of view. Think of Plato as a noble, advocating the nobility's right to rule Athens, locked in a struggle with a group who wished, in a more democratic spirit, to widen the base of government so that more Athenians might participate in government. Think, further, of Athens as a city in which it was expected that anyone advocating a point of view must be willing and able to back it up with argument.

In one kind of argument which the nobles pressed against the democrats, they characterized the mass of free men as a rabble which knows nothing, which conducts its affairs, and can be expected to conduct the affairs of state, in accordance with its desires rather than its reason. Having no knowledge with which to govern, goes the nobles' argument, the rabble has no way of deciding on a course of action except by means of the vote; a vote, however, is not a measure of the rabble's knowledge, but of its strongest or most pervasive desires and appetites. The ignorant democratic rabble is like a beast conflictedly tugged first this way and then that by its unbridled vote-hungry appetites.

Think now of a reply by a democrat that challenged the assumptions in Plato's argument against the democratic point of view. Plato assumed, goes the reply, that there really is knowledge about what is best for the city-state, and he assumed, further, that we are able to say what this knowledge is, and he assumed, still further, that we are able to determine who possesses this knowledge. Until these assumptions can be shown to be tenable, argues the democrat, we have no assurance that there is any knowledge which the nobility might claim as its exclusive possession. Until that has been shown, the best guide to civic policy is the wishes of the citizens. What is more humane and more just than to give first place to those wishes that a vote shows are wished by most men?

Think now of Plato, familiar with the democratic challenge to his assumptions, trying to spin out a theory which will show his assumptions to be tenable. One way to meet the challenge is to claim that there exist special objects of knowledge, the Ideas, which exist independently of any person's thoughts or wishes; that knowledge of these Ideas is gained only after rigorous training and by dialectical ascent; that this ascent is akin to the progress of rational argument exhibited in Plato's dialogues; and that only trained philosophers having gone through the dialectical process possess knowledge of the Ideas; hence, concludes Plato, if civic affairs are handled best by those who know, then we had better make our rulers philosopher-kings, a truly noble class, élite, knowledgeable, and above democratic excesses.

I have tried, in a brief sketch, to indicate how philosophy comes into existence, how it is squeezed into existence by the jaws of controversy mashing down on matters of political importance to persons living in a society that prides itself on reasoning its way to community. Controversy squeezed the Ideas out of Plato, those metaphysical jewels of the nobility.

Philosophy remains vital by being sustained in the same way. Philosophy can be revitalized here in our cities if philosophers practice their profession in the agora as well as in the academy, discoursing with citizens on matters of importance to them, reasoning their way to community.

By placing themselves in the jaws of current controversy, philosophers will make philosophy currently relevant instead of historically revered. In this essay, I have tried to find the jaws of our time so citizens will know where they must place themselves to have philosophy squeezed out of them. I have found our philosophic jaws on either side of the gap between the first and second arc of our return to Eden. The squeeze is on; to save ourselves, we have got to philosophize ourselves into a new form of life and society in which, I have argued, concinnation is the chief vocation. If professional philosophers and the vital underground cooperate in brightening the fires of illumination, we may once again see a Golden Age and feel the excitement of living in it because we participate in it.

Wide participation in philosophy, realistically, can occur only at the spoken level. Written philosophy, as I said, will seem more important than spoken philosophizing if the aim of philosophy is thought to be the production of doctrine, as if philosophers were to bring down from guru-high mountain tops inscribed stone-stiff tablets as Moses did. The day to day life of a community is carried on at a more flexible verbal level. Philosophy can be a part of that life only if it too is verbal. We who love philosophy must not consent to its being scholasticized and petrified in print.

Philosophy, when most vital, is a verbal activity. Its aim is to produce concinnity, not doctrine. To produce concinnity, we must change men. Philosophizing is an effort of people to change each other by rational discourse; it is a mutual attempt to concinnate their many conflicting individual and class points of view into a social point of view. Philosophizing, not philosophy: The accent is on action. Throw off your chains of publication! Gather ye faggots for the fires of illumination, fires quick to dim without their feast of faggots.

Philosophizing will not come at once to all in our city. But if art comes to all, philosophy will soon attend it, for art, when detrivialized, is foreplay to philosophy, a loving prelude to communal concinnation. Let me explain this.

I argued earlier that art may be detrivialized if it is used as an instrument of moral power. It becomes a moral instrument when it is used to infuse another's point of view into our understanding. I compared points of view to chapters in a novel; when a complementary, diverse chapter is added to others, the novel is enlarged; when a complementary, diverse point of view is added to our own, our personal understanding is enlarged.

We may have an enlarged personal understanding because we simultaneously hold several points of view in our understanding; still those several points of view may not be consistent with each other. Your facts may not be consistent with my facts, even though I understand what your facts are; my interests may conflict with your interests, even though momentarily I feel all the passion of your interests; your moral ideals may be my moral vices, even though I understand how you justify them. Though an enlarged understanding is a valuable achievement, it is not the ultimate achievement. The ultimate achievement is the philosophical creation of a social point of view, a point of view purged of conflict and inconsistency.

Philosophy thrives on controversy. There is no controversy unless persons understand conflicting points of view. Art, by providing this understanding, provokes the tongue of philosophy. Since philosophizing is the discursive process of concinnating conflicting points of view into a social point of view, and since art amplifies those conflicts, art, decentralized and detrivialized, will seduce us into that ultimate concinnatory activity we call philosophy.

A society too large for extensive verbal exchange can never be a philosophical democracy. It can be at best a political democracy. If concinnation be our proper vocation, and if philosophy is the noblest concinnatory act of all, our destiny can be fulfilled only in a city state. Only a city is small enough to sustain philosophical democracy. If you must cling to nations, at least demand of them that they serve this one function: Promote a climate which will nourish a collection of philosophical, civic democracies.

It is not too late to lead the good life. Philosophy forks off the road at all points.

The Beginning

APPENDIX

ON THE IDEA OF AN ART FORCE

Taik uppe the Muskett of Arte.
The Enymy is uppe pon uss.
　　　　—FANEBIUS PERLYNG

⚗　⚗　⚗

IN THE PREFACE to this essay, and in other places herein, I have said why I decline to supply concrete details about the ideal city, or about how cities may free themselves from nations, or about the new institutions that will be needed if we are to pass from a dominant work vocation to concinnation. Lest the reader, nevertheless, think this essay hopelessly utopian and out of touch with practical reality, I add this appendix indicating my actual, practical attempt to create a new institution—a neighborhood arts program—in an United States city—San Francisco. Perhaps a brief description of its inception, purposes, and nature will lend this essay the reality orientation that will give it a credence that reaches past logical, theoretical possibility.

The inception of this essay occurred in a series of philosophy classes at San Francisco State College. In them, we first addressed ourselves to the way in which liberal arts students could actively improve the city's life by utilizing the skills and the learning acquired in school. The application of the physical and social sciences was obvious enough; there are many institutions developed by our society through which physical and social science students could readily channel their civic efforts. But there did not seem to be any such institutions for students of the arts, and the arts were what the majority of the philosophy class students were interested in utilizing in an attempt to improve San Francisco. They also wanted to create interesting and relevant employment for themselves and to overcome the uselessness of the arts; these goals did not appear attainable without the creation of a new institution.

You might think that museums, symphonies, galleries, dance companies, little theaters, and so forth, are existing institutions through which students of the arts could channel their expertise, energy, idealism, and knowledge. This possibility was quickly eliminated by the students. These institutions' remoteness from the people was painfully obvious to them because most of them had seen the Teatro Campesino, a troupe of farm workers turned actors, headed by a professional actor. This troupe played in the fields, not in concert halls and theaters, to migrant farm workers that Cesar Chavez was trying to organize into an effective union; they played in Spanish and English. Their aim was to expose to farm workers the causes for their conditions, to make them conscious of their employers' exploitation of them, to stir them to anger and action, and to propose unionization as the only solution to their miserable conditions of work and life. Broadly played theater vigorously depicting farm workers, sheriffs, landlords, priests, and union organizers were the only mobile means the union had available to reach workers who either didn't read, or didn't have time to read, or didn't have the money to buy books, or were too exhausted to inform themselves. The Teatro Campesino had a stirring message, an obvious moral purpose; it utilized people untrained in the arts, who heroically had to defy arrests, resist beatings, and overcome harassment. Most of the establishment art institutions looked pale and trivial to my students in comparison to this courageous, morally useful theater troupe.

They recognized that art is not now a political, moral, or social instrument of any moment in our cities. It is neither a weapon for the radicals, nor a platform for moderates, nor a bulwark for the conservatives. It functions primarily, except for some artists who have carried the flag for the young, as entertainment. The students saw that internal reform of established art institutions is a hopeless endeavor because they are controlled chiefly by entrepreneurs who must present a homogenized product suitable for a wide enough audience to make a good "gate" or "classic" works approved as "good" or "great" by influential critics. There is, too, the *avant garde*, who carry the banner of the new and "difficult" against the ramparts of popular entertainment and safe academics, but they are a small, brave, isolated in-group who simply are not going to create a broad social revolution with their works.

Neither mere entertainment nor the classics nor the *avant garde* are adequate for transforming art into a civic power. The usual mode of packaging, dispensing, and creating art has to be altered. Establishment art is in search of a wider audience. Instead of more Sol Hurok, All-American, star-touting public relations to entice more people into the audience, we must resist the downtown, art center, museum mentality that seems to have hypnotized New York, Los Angeles, and Washington. The erection of their parthenons of culture are desperate attempts to preserve the value of downtown real estate and to pied pipe suburbanites back into being urbanites, if only for a few ticket spree nights of the year.

According to the philosophy classes' analyses, the composer, playwright, choreographer, poet, novelist, screenwriter, painter, and sculptor have to respond to the audience which patronizes them if they are to remain solvent while practicing their art. As long as that audience has to pay the prices now current and has to go to the palaces now provided, the artists will be creating works for a small percentage of the people. Major orchestras, opera companies, and repertory theaters could not exist without private and public endowments. Seasons are short. The economic condition of the establishment arts is no secret. They are desperate for a larger audience. But all they have to sell most people is participation in prestige. No amount of public relations can make most people believe that anything so trivial in their present lives has so much prestige that they really can't live the good life without patronizing the establishment art offerings.

Art will never have a wide, ardent audience unless it is relevant to citizens' lives, unless it becomes a political and social instrument for them. This means that art must incorporate the points of view of citizens, it must relate their life knowledge, their aspirations, beefs, angers, hopes, ideals, and desires as the Teatro Campesino did. And it must be made easily available to those whom it must change, which includes all of us. And better that it should be crude and honest than slick and false.

A point of view is a first-person thing before it is a third-person thing. An artist who does not have personal acquaintance with a point of view cannot convincingly present it replete with the right accent and emotions. An artist seldom can create works with first-person authenticity who does not live among the people whose point of view he wishes to present and who does not expose his work to the critical pressure of those holding that point of view. An audience is a creative force; it forces revision, honesty, heat, relevance, economy, fairness; it supplies substance. The arts are a form of address.

It was evident to the students and me that there are some serious, practical problems for the arts in the United States. There are economic and distribution problems; the power of art is nullified, its relevance is absent, and there is little honesty left in its practitioners, appreciators, or salesmen. These are problems of such size and complexity that they cannot be solved by individuals acting alone; they are problems that require concerted action. Nor can these problems be solved by cosmetic, reformist attempts at "rededication" of the arts; further, of least help and most harm would be federal subsidization of the arts; that just means using the tax money of people who do not now relate to the arts to pay the costs of the kind of art that appeals to the present, narrow, established patronage referred to earlier. These problems will not be solved except through the creation of a new institution, an art force, if you will.

The classes' proposal comes, I hope, as no surprise; we decided that a city art force should be a neighborhood arts program. It would provide for the decentralization of art into the city's neighborhoods and would call, not for central arts palaces, but neighborhood arts and cultural centers. With city funding, and additional money from local foundations, a neighborhood arts program would seek for the existing talent and groups in the city's neighborhoods, make and keep available a list of the talent and groups for the use of neighborhoods wanting to sponsor programs, locate free public facilities and low cost private facilities in the neighborhoods for programs and art classes, help publicize arts events, organize "seed" shows, provide a stage truck for people to use in the parks and on the streets, lend audio, light, and tool equipment, produce posters and advertising for neighborhoods, provide instructors and class spaces for young people and children, encourage arts that reflected the culture of the neighborhood from which the persons and groups came, and sponsor art fairs in neighborhoods.

Through political action, we did succeed in persuading the Mayor and Supervisors to set up and fund a neighborhood arts program. Local foundations have contributed funds for the past several years as well; to date, several million dollars have been expended on the program. The Supervisors' budget hearings have never drawn the crowds nor the interest that the neighborhood arts budget hearings did; the people poured in from every neighborhood in the city. Voices cracked, tears swelled, and paeans of praise flowed in loving regard for the program. The people were beginning to feel that government would allow them to do something for themselves and that they could help determine policy for at least one governmental institution. We saw that a rejuvenation of a sense of community suitable to a modern city is possible and practicable. The city began to move toward an intra-city exchange circuit; neighborhoods began to exchange programs and began to acquire understanding.

The original impetus of the program has been nearly destroyed by incompetence, political chicanery, and lack of vision, but a point has been made about the viability of an art force. Until the whole city government as it now exists escapes the influence of the nation, the state, and big money interests and is totally reorganized, no single governmental institution can by itself bring about the millenium. Reformism obviously is no substitute for revolution, whether that revolution be peaceful or violent.

The establishment of a neighborhood arts program was politically possible because a bond issue calling for construction of new and renovation of existing buildings serving established art was defeated. The main cause of the defeat was the people's desire that something be done for "unestablished" art before more money was to be spent on rich men's playthings. The financial movers of the city decided that giving the people a neighborhood arts program would be good insurance; if the neighborhoods got something, then next time the bond issue came up, they would vote for it. A poll showed that voters heavily favored neighborhood art centers over a central palace. This is not surprising. The city provides schools for those who want to learn, libraries for those who want to read, tennis courts, baseball diamonds, soccer fields, and swimming pools for those who want to play tennis, baseball, soccer, and who want to swim; it provides an opera house for those who want symphonies and opera; it builds museums and buys art; it provides parks for those who want to play, sit, picnic, and walk. Therefore, it is consistent with public policy to build, fund, and staff neighborhood art centers, and to encourage those who evisage a significant role for the arts in our cities. It is consistent with public policy to staff them with people who aspire to make the moral power of art available to all who wish to take part. It is consistent with public policy to create an art force.

A curious result occurred as the program grew in success and acceptance; instead of inclining people more favorably toward a bond issue for a central arts palace, it turned them against it and made them more desirous of neighborhood arts centers. Once they had learned that art need not be trivial and that it can be dangerous, they came to see the program as an instrument of power. So did the financial minions and their politicians; the sabotage of the program dates from the second poll showing that the program was not favorably influencing the voters toward another bond issue.

It is clear to me, however, that the days of central arts palaces are numbered; neighborhood arts are in. The idea has caught on in several cities, and it is only a matter of time when cities will begin constructing neighborhood arts centers. It will be difficult to spike the musket of art when people recognize that an art force will do more to help attain the good life than a police force will.

Given the problems of the arts that our classes isolated, the purposes of a neighborhood arts program were identifiable by reference to those problems. These purposes guided the determination of the program I outlined above, such as locating and listing talent and free public space and providing a stage truck for use in parks and streets. These purposes are practicable, not utopian; they are relatable to actual, specific, programmatic action which at one time actually took place.

One practical purpose of a city-supported neighborhood arts program is to address the economics of art. It can provide reasonable-cost programs to people not now attracted to the arts; it can provide jobs and income for artists who would staff the neighborhood arts centers; it can provide opportunities and places for people to perform and practice their art who would not otherwise be able to do so because of prohibitive costs and small audiences.

A second purpose of a neighborhood arts program is to alter the distribution of art. We found that an unsuspectedly large reservoir of talent resides in every neighborhood; ordinarily, their material never gets distributed; present *laissez faire* production and distribution methods ballyhoo and risk capital on only those things that the agents think will sell to the now narrow taste range of the few who spend money on the arts. Perhaps most importantly, different neighborhoods would begin to learn about each other's point of view and start on the road to reaching a social point of view if the neighborhood arts were to reflect the people and if a neighborhood circuit were established enabling the neighborhoods to exchange programs. It is the distribution of viewpoints that would be accomplished by a distribution of the arts through this kind of program.

A third purpose of a neighborhood arts program is to release the power of art. That art has power, and that this power is of a kind that changes people is shown by the fact that people in power have always advocated censorship of the arts—and this includes people in power in all forms of government. My argument in this essay entails that city government has an essential, moral task: It should be an instrument that promotes the unity of a city. This is a more important task for it than providing garbage and sewage services; the latter can be provided by private business, but private business requiring profit as their survival imperative cannot be the instrument for unifying a city because businesses must promote primarily private, not public, interests; further, private business cannot tolerate public participation and still be private. The aim of making a profit through private management is antithetical to the aim of unifying a city; only a non-profit oriented, publicly, controlled body (government?) can be an instrument of unification. I have argued in this essay that art has moral power; you have read my argument that moral power should be put to use in moving citizens toward a social point of view; a social point of view, a social understanding, is the relation that unifies neighborhoods into a city; therefore, a government seriously trying to carry out the moral task of unifying a city should count among its institutions an art force, a neighborhood arts program. The power of art should be used for moral, public ends, not merely for individualistic private ends as at present.

A fourth purpose of a neighborhood arts program is to recover the relevance of art. I do not need to expand on this for those who have read the next-to-last chapter of this essay on the detrivialization of the arts. I only repeat that art that reflects the life knowledge of the people will not be irrelevantly trivial.

A fifth purpose of a neighborhood arts program is to reinspirt the devotees of art with honesty. A world pandering almost exclusively to commercial interests has permuted artists into hustlers. Providing an alternative to commercial exploitation is the only way aesthetic hustlers can return *en masse* to being artists. There is a close affinity between art and morality even when art is at its most aesthetic, as both Santayana and David Prall pointed out; the stench of filth can give an urgency to eliminating poverty. A neighborhood arts program that is willing to open its channels to creative artists who need the moral criticism of their neighbors to enforce honesty, will make hustling unnecessary.

Having spent a good part of several years conceiving, working toward the realization, and keeping active in the programmatic evolution of the San Francisco neighborhood arts program, I appreciate the practical problems of creating a new institution. I also came to appreciate the ultimate futility of piece-meal reform; we shall have to overthrow the nation and establish city-states finally in order to arrest our own and society's descent into the purgatory of alienation.

A purposeful journey cannot be undertaken without a destination in mind. This essay has been my attempt to envision a new destination for man. It is also an attempt to place the arts, decentralized, into a larger, more complex, theoretical, ideal, human perspective, that is, into a philosophical perspective. I hope that this appendix gives some clue that I have paid a few dues and am entitled to have you read or think about my essay as if it is not totally devoid of practical wisdom and that I have as much respect for the achievable as for the dreamable.

Index